Golden Girls

Golden Girls was first staged by the Royal Shakespeare Company at The Other Place, Stratford-upon-Avon, in summer 1984.

Golden Girls is 'a topically Olympic account of women training for the 100 metres relay . . . it's far and away the best new play the RSC have done since *Good* and also the best thing I've seen in ten years at The Other Place . . . Far from a latterday *Chariots of Fire*, it's really about the impossibility of running clean or free in a world where sexism and racism and sponsorship and drugs have already taken their toll on a sporting ethic . . . I have a feeling the play will be around on both sides of the Atlantic for a long time to come'.

Sheridan Morley, *Punch*

Louise Page was born in London in 1955 and at the age of five moved to Sheffield. She read Drama and Theatre Arts at Birmingham University and, in 1979, she became Yorkshire Television's Fellow in Drama and Television at the University of Sheffield. Her stage plays include *Want-Ad* (Birmingham Arts Lab, 1977; ICA, 1979); *Lucy* (Bristol New Vic Studio, 1979); *Tissue* (Birmingham Repertory Theatre, 1978; ICA, 1978; adapted for Radio 4, 1979); *Hearing* (Birmingham Repertory Theatre, 1979); *Flaws* (Sheffield University Drama Studio, 1980); *Housewives* (Derby Playhouse, 1981, a Radio/Theatre production); *Salonika* (Royal Court Theatre Upstairs, 1982; winner of the George Devine Award); *Falkland Sound/Voices de Malvinas* (Royal Court Theatre Upstairs and on tour, 1983-4); *Real Estate* (Tricycle Theatre, London, 1984) and *Golden Girls* (Royal Shakespeare Company, The Other Place, Stratford-upon-Avon, 1984). *Beauty and the Beast* (jointly commissioned by The Women's Playhouse Trust and Methuen) opened at the Liverpool Playhouse in November 1985 before transferring to the Old Vic, London in December 1985. She has also written for radio and television.

The front cover photo is by Donald Cooper and shows Josette Simon as Dorcas in the RSC's 1984 production. The photograph of Louise Page on the back cover is by Sarah Ainslie.

LOUISE PAGE

Golden Girls

A METHUEN PAPERBACK

For Vanessa with my love

A METHUEN MODERN PLAY

First published in Great Britain in 1985 by Methuen London
Ltd., 11 New Fetter Lane, London EC4P 4EE and in the
United States of America by Methuen Inc., 722 Third Avenue,
New York, NY 10017
Reprinted 1987
© 1985 by Louise Page
Set in IBM 10pt Journal by Words & Pictures Ltd, London
SE19
Printed in Great Britain

British Library Cataloguing in Publication Data

Page, Louise
  Golden girls
  I. Title
  822'.914   PR6066.A3/

  ISBN 0-413-57960-3

This version of *Golden Girls* was first presented by the Royal Shakespeare Company at The Other Place, Stratford-upon-Avon, on 20 June, 1984, with the following cast:

DORCAS ABLEMAN, *black athlete*	Josette Simon
MURIEL FARR, *black athlete*	Alphonsia Emmanuel
PAULINE PETERSON, *white athlete*	Katherine Rogers
SUE KINDER, *blonde white athlete*	Kate Buffery
JANET MORRIS, *black athlete*	Cathy Tyson
MIKE BASSETT, *white athlete*	Kenneth Branagh
LACES MACKENZIE, *coach*	Jimmy Yuill
VIVIEN BLACKWOOD, *doctor*	Jennifer Piercey
NOËL KINDER, *Sue Kinder's father*	George Raistrick
HILARY DAVENPORT, *sponsor*	Polly James
TOM BILLBOW, *journalist*	Derek Crewe
HOTEL PORTER, *white*	Norman Henry
THE GOLDEN GIRL, *everything the name suggests*	Jan Revere

Directed by Barry Kyle
Designed by Kit Surrey
Music by Ilona Sekacz
Lighting by Wayne Dowdeswell

Acknowledgement
Special thanks to Ron Pickering for the sports commentary on page 61.

ACT ONE

Scene One

A pile of luggage in a hotel lobby. Enter TOM. *He looks at the luggage. Enter the* PORTER *with more luggage.*

PORTER. You think they'd have the energy to do their own fetching and carrying. Bloody athletes. When Sheffield Wednesday were here they were gentlemen. (*He goes.*)

    TOM *looks at the luggage. He turns over the tags on the bags.*

    TOM *goes.*

    Enter MURIEL. *She limps to the bags and sits down. She begins to unbandage her foot. Enter the* PORTER.

PORTER. Gentlemen! (*He goes.*)

    MURIEL *begins to flex her foot. Enter* VIVIEN.

VIVIEN. Right, let's have a look. How's that feel?

MURIEL. O.K.

    VIVIEN *moves the foot.* MURIEL *winces.*

VIVIEN. I'll strap it up as tightly as I can now and have another look in the morning.

MURIEL. Should I have an X-ray?

VIVIEN. It's a ligament.

MURIEL. I pass casualty.

VIVIEN. If I thought you needed an X-ray you'd have had one by now. (VIVIEN *bangs on her chest indicating where* MURIEL *is to put her foot.*)

No need to kick me in the teeth. (*She starts to strap*.) Doesn't seem too bad.

MURIEL. No?

VIVIEN. A sprained ligament. Hardly the end of the world. It could have been your Achilles tendon.

MURIEL. I've only been out twice before.

VIVIEN. You've been unusually lucky.

MURIEL. Age is catching up on me, isn't it?

VIVIEN. If your times are good enough, keep on running. You ought to be pleased with your own event.

MURIEL (*shrugs*). When did you give up?

VIVIEN. When I couldn't go to Helsinki. The longest women's race there was the 200. Not my event. It was Finland for the Olympics or Charing Cross Hospital. Can you flex that?

MURIEL *tries but can't*.

Good. Medicine was tough for a woman then. They still had the quota system. I knew I wouldn't get a medal and I wanted a degree. I had to take myself seriously. It was a different world. Terrific fun. Then the four minute mile was cracked and it all seemed to get serious. Perhaps we were just younger then.

Enter LACES.

LACES. I've given them the hurry up. Is it the problem she's pretending it is?

VIVIEN. There's a lot of flexibility. I'll have another look at it in the morning. (*To* MURIEL.) There's no point pushing yourself for a situation you can't save.

LACES. Dorcas is pretty mad about it. She's gone off somewhere.

MURIEL. What she's mad about is Sue's time in the 200. To be beaten in that and have Sue blow it in the relay.

VIVIEN. You can't blame it all on Sue. The German girls have really got it together.

MURIEL. We can get it together.

LACES. Then why didn't you?

MURIEL *shrugs.*

Vivien?

VIVIEN. I deal with bodies not minds.

LACES. Some ideas must have gone through your head.

VIVIEN. They believed absolutely they could do it.

LACES. And that gave them the upper hand?

VIVIEN. Amongst other things.

LACES. Oh! You think they are?

VIVIEN. If they are it's nothing that's shown up yet.

MURIEL. Common gossip in the changing-rooms.

LACES. Hazzard a guess.

VIVIEN. A hundred and one things. All sorts of drugs they could be taking and flushing out of their system before the tests.

LACES. Name them.

VIVIEN. There have been some interesting reports on a drug called di — the shorthand name for it is hydromel. After the stuff the Romans used to dope their horses but this is new. Derived from the embryos of rats.

MURIEL. Yuk!

VIVIEN. It speeds up the motor processes. It's already on the black market here. But I can't see us ever being allowed to prescribe it. Then again it could all be weights.

MURIEL. We use weights.

VIVIEN. It's not a couple of nights a week sort of muscle.

MURIEL. Thank goodness.

VIVIEN. You have to decide if you want to be a winner or a star.

Pause.

You can't have East German times without the East German system. And they've got the lot, from the kudos of the sports personality to the chemistry. We haven't got it together here —

there's no money.

LACES. Ortolan?

VIVIEN. A drop in the ocean. All it buys is tracksuits for the girls and a bit of your time. If I were to charge for this you couldn't afford it.

MURIEL. I'm sorry.

VIVIEN. That's the system. Why should you apologise?

Pause.

LACES. If I could get the money would you come in — full time?

VIVIEN. It doesn't happen in this country.

LACES. If I made it?

MURIEL. You sound like the fairy godmother in Adidas.

LACES. If the money was there, Vivien?

VIVIEN. Ortolan isn't going to pay for a team doctor.

LACES. Why not?

VIVIEN. O.K. Find me the pay cheque.

LACES. How much?

VIVIEN. A lot.

LACES. The love of the game?

VIVIEN. Times have changed. Mine is the leather suitcase. It's a business now.

MURIEL. Is it O.K. for me to phone George?

VIVIEN. As long as you don't put your full weight on it.

MURIEL *goes to the phone.* LACES *watches her go.*

LACES. Technically she's the best we've got. If she could just understand that. She needs Dorcas's killer instinct. She can break records in training. She could do in competition if she'd just believe in herself.

VIVIEN. Perhaps she doesn't want to.

LACES. Why not?

VIVIEN. Frightened.

LACES. How can you be frightened of winning?

VIVIEN. It sets you apart.

It's also called being a woman.

LACES. Don't! Don't! Don't!

VIVIEN. I am trying to explain. You could at least listen.

LACES. Sue wants to win. Pauline wants to win. Dorcas wants it more than the whole world. So being a woman is hardly a hypothesis. You're hardly a shrinking violet.

VIVIEN. I'm a doctor. People have to believe in me. People like Ortolan.

MURIEL. Have you got a dialling code booklet?

PORTER. Bulawayo is it?

MURIEL. Buxton.

The PORTER *grudgingly finds her the code book.*

Enter MIKE.

LACES. Found her?

MIKE. No.

LACES. Any ideas?

MIKE. No.

LACES. Your time wasn't bad.

MIKE. Hers was.

LACES. All her stuff here?

MIKE. Think so.

LACES. I'm not waiting once we're all here. It's up to you if you come with us or hang on for her.

MIKE. I've a tutorial at ten.

LACES. On?

MIKE. Community access to educational sports facilities.

VIVIEN *looks at her watch and yawns.*

VIVIEN. I've got a surgery.

MIKE. I'll go and give them a shout.

LACES. I've tried that. Progress!

Enter NOËL.

LACES. Where's Sue?

NOËL. Taking her Qwells.

LACES. You know they stay in the system.

NOËL. Didn't take them on the way down.

LACES. She managed.

NOËL. Empty stomach. No point in tempting fate.

MIKE. I'll get the others. (*He goes.*)

LACES. You haven't seen Dorcas?

NOËL. No.

LACES. This time I really am going without her.

VIVIEN. Laces, you can't.

LACES. She's been warned.

VIVIEN. You can't leave her here in the middle of the night.

LACES. Can't I?

NOËL. Teach her her lesson.

Enter SUE.

MURIEL. You look as if you should be going out on the town.

SUE. Thanks.

LACES. You've checked your room?

SUE. Pauline's having a last look.

LACES. Good, then we can go.

NOËL. I'm ready.

SUE. Please Dad.

LACES. It's been a lousy day. Let's just get home. (NOËL *and* LACES *look at the map.*)

NOËL. The sooner I get to my bed the better.

LACES. That goes for all of us.

VIVIEN. Are you always travel sick?

SUE. Better safe than sorry.

VIVIEN. Have you ever tried ginger for it.

SUE. Ginger?

VIVIEN. It might help.

MURIEL. Sounds old wives to me.

VIVIEN. Placebo effect. You'd be surprised how often something patients belive in will work.

SUE. Not now you've told me.

VIVIEN. It might be worth trying.

NOËL. What might?

VIVIEN. Ginger.

MURIEL. To stop her feeling sick on the bus.

NOËL. Sounds like mumbo jumbo to me.

   (*Enter* PAULINE.)

PAULINE. I've lost Split Second.

NOËL. That bloody bear.

LACES. You've looked in your room?

PAULINE. Of course.

VIVIEN. Your bag.

   (PAULINE *looks in it*.)

PAULINE. No. He's been stolen. Some bloody fan.

SUE. Who'd steal Split Second. He's got mange.

PAULINE. He hasn't.

LACES. If they find him they can send him on.

PAULINE. I'm not going without him. I can't run without him.

NOËL. In my day luck depended on how you tied your shoelaces.

PAULINE. I can't.

NOËL. Sure he wasn't lost before the relay?

SUE. Dad!

NOËL. Sorry. Silly joke. Late at night.

VIVIEN. Where did you have him last?

PAULINE. He came down to the track. Then we came back here. I had a bath, dinner, then the bar.

MURIEL. You had him at dinner.

LACES. You looked in the bar?

PAULINE. I'm not going till we find him.

LACES. You want to spend another night in this place?

PAULINE. I know you don't care.

VIVIEN *crosses to desk.*

VIVIEN. Excuse me —

PORTER. Half past ten it was you were supposed to be going.

VIVIEN. They've lost something.

PORTER. Every race they've run.

VIVIEN. Have you had anything handed in. A toy. A children's toy?

Enter MIKE.

PORTER. That Mike Bassett?

VIVIEN. Yes.

PORTER. He do autographs?

VIVIEN. Yes.

PORTER. Might be worth getting I suppose.

VIVIEN. It's a sort of bear — with a ribbon.

The PORTER *begins to throw up lost property with bad grace. All watch. He holds up Split Second.* PAULINE *rushes for him jumping over cases as she goes.*

PORTER. You should try going in for the hurdles.

LACES. Yippee. Right. Let's go.

Variously they claim their baggage and go — MIKE *last.*

PORTER. Your autograph worth anything?

MIKE. Sorry?

PORTER. You know, your name?

MIKE *shrugs.*

Might as well — eh — just in case. Never know what might happen in the future.

MIKE *writes in the book. As he's about to go, enter* DORCAS *with a laundry bag.*

MIKE. Where the hell have you been?

DORCAS *drops the washing.*

I was worried.

Enter NOËL.

NOËL. Will you get your bum on this bus. (*He glares at* DORCAS.) Go walkabout did we? (*He goes.*)

MIKE. Well?

DORCAS. The drier wouldn't work.

Enter TOM BILLBOW.

MIKE. Let's get home.

PORTER (*to* DORCAS). Can you write? (*She looks at him.*) You know. Writing? (*He mimes. She puts out her hand for the pen. She writes her name.*) You have to put more than that. Don't suppose they have autographs were you come from. You have to put 'to Denis and Diana' — (*She does.*) Then they usually put best wishes or good luck or something.

(*She does.*)

You'll get the hang of it. And the date. (*She does.*) Ta. (*The* PORTER *looks at the autograph.*)

How come you don't run for Jamaica?

DORCAS. I don't need the tan.

Pause.

MIKE. Let's get home. (*He goes.*)

TOM. The name Dorcas — means gazelle doesn't it?

DORCAS. Yes. (*She picks up the washing. She goes.*)

Blackout.

Scene Two

Darkness. Out of the darkness the sound of a runner running. Lights up to pre-dawn. The runner is SUE.

SUE. You know which direction you're going in at home. The north slopes and the south. The south slopes have posh houses. The ones that get the sunlight. There's a saying there about downhill being uphill but it's all running on the flat here. No hills. No view out over it all. You could go on and on. The time was when I thought there must be something would make me stop before the horizon. A tree, mountain, mole hill. Some obstacle. Nothing. Just further and further to go. On and on towards the sun. (*She continues to run.*)

Enter NOËL *with a stopwatch.*

NOËL. Bugger!

The floodlights come on. NOËL *times the stopwatch to his own watch, counting. Enter* LACES.

LACES. Morning.

NOËL *nods. The stopwatch is obviously broken.*

NOËL. Can you lend us a stopwatch? This is buggered. Forty-two seconds and then stops dead.

LACES. Give it to the East Germans.

NOËL. Glad somebody can laugh.

LACES. They'd make no bones about it being a record attempt. The psyching was brilliant.

NOËL. Sue knows not to let a thing like that throw her.

LACES. If you're psyched for long enough, well enough, you've got no chance of winning.

NOËL. She knows she's got twenty-one seconds in her legs.

LACES. If she doesn't over do it.

NOËL. I know what her legs can do.

LACES. I think you should watch it. Lay up a bit. Do you think she should be out this morning?

NOËL. Why's today different?

MIKE *runs across the stage.*

LACES. She's run four races in two days.

NOËL. Sue knows how much effort you have to put in before you dare hope for a bit of magic.

LACES. And if there's no magic?

NOËL. You do without.

MIKE. Morning.

LACES. Morning.

NOËL. It's wasting her to use her at less than 200.

LACES. Do you want me to drop her from the squad?

NOËL. You've got us over a barrel. She needs the facilities.

LACES. I'd like it back. (*He gives* NOËL *the stopwatch.*)

NOËL. Ta.

LACES. Tell her not to push it too much. (LACES *jogs off.*)

NOËL. One minute recovery.

SUE. I hate running tired. Running with your mind, not your body. Waiting for the moment when the two fuse. Knowing that some days they won't. That all it will have been is putting on your tee-shirt, your tracksuit. Tying your laces. The routine. Other days the most perfect, perfect thing. No thoughts at all. Absolute symmetry in your head. Like the perfect races when you know just what to do. Not yesterday, a ragbag of tactics and strategy. I could feel the clock in my head. Time running out. And knowing every fraction of a second that there wasn't going to be a moment which lasted for ever.

NOËL *shows her the time on the stopwatch.*

NOËL. Again.

SUE. No.

NOËL. I said again.

SUE. No.

NOËL. Don't take that tone with me, miss.

SUE. I can't better that.

NOËL. You can and you will.

Pause.

You're a winner, love. You just have to get it together. Then it won't be living in a camper for decent facilities. You'll have everything you deserve. A pretty girl like you, Sue. Think about it.

SUE. It's impossible.

NOËL. It's not, love. I've shown you it's not. You're a winner, love. From the day you were born.

SUE. Don't throw that at me.

NOËL. You were a winner then.

SUE. Don't tell me that.

NOËL. She'd be proud.

SUE. Not listening.

NOËL. Me proud then. Crack it and you can stay in bed for ever.

SUE. Who wants to stay in bed in a camper?

NOËL. If you want everything they've got here.

Pause.

What do you want?

She shakes her head.

We'll go home. I'll drive you twenty miles there and back

everyday. But you still won't get the half of what they've got here.

SUE. I can't run any faster for you, Dad —

NOËL. Then run it for yourself. Come on. Again.

She runs off. He watches her. LACES *jogs back on.*

She could have gold, couldn't she? Real gold.

LACES. There won't be anything if she over-does it.

NOËL. She wasn't allowed to run her own event without running the relay.

LACES. It's the same for all four of them.

NOËL. It's hardly the same amount of glory.

LACES. Muriel, Pauline, Dorcas, Sue — I'm not saying that they're the most perfect team — yet.

NOËL. Certainly weren't yesterday —

LACES. But they could get so near. So exciting. Certainly be the best there's been in this country for a very long time. I know it's not peace and light between the four of them but when they're on that track with the baton — they could be —

NOËL. I don't like the word perfect.

LACES. But nearly that. I don't want Sue to let it slip through her her fingers. Not now they've come this far together.

NOËL. You don't think she's any good on her own?

LACES. She's superb.

NOËL *is pleased.*

That's why I need her in the relay. She's got that power for that first leg.
I know it's been hardest for her. That she's giving up a bed and bathroom back home. But if she can run the way she does living in a camper, with the money that's coming for the team from Ortolan, it could be a different world for her.

NOËL. Tea?

LACES. No, haven't finished.

NOËL *pours some tea.*

Wish I'd got it together the way you have. (LACES *runs off.*)

Enter MURIEL *and* PAULINE.

MURIEL. It wasn't your fault.

PAULINE. It was.

MURIEL. The stupid idiot was in the wrong lane.

LACES (*shouting to them*). Don't you dare try anything on that ankle until Dr Blackwood's seen it.

MURIEL (*shouting*). I know.
The thing you mustn't do is panic. Slowing down's a fatal mistake. If you stall, switch off the engine and start again.

PAULINE. I'll never get the hang of it.

MURIEL. You will.

NOËL *comes past them with* SUE'S *things and some tea.*

Morning.

NOËL. Morning.

PAULINE. You should park your camper up here. You could make a fortune from bacon sandwiches.

NOËL. Might end up doing that yet. (*He gestures to* SUE.) Come on, get your things, have a shower. (*He goes with* SUE')

PAULINE *and* MURIEL *start to stretch and warm up.*

LACES *is doing press-ups. Enter* TOM.

TOM (*to* NOËL). Morning.

PAULINE. ⎱ Morning.
MURIEL. ⎰

TOM. Keep thinking I should get fit. Lose a bit of this. Had a girlfriend once, bought me a tracksuit. Think it was a hint. I find the mornings difficult.

LACES. Can I help, Tom?

TOM *gets down to look at* LACES.

TOM. Laces Mackenzie?

LACES. Yes.

TOM. Used to be a great fan.

LACES. Thanks.

TOM. They say you have a lot of trouble with your knee.

LACES. Some days.

>MURIEL *is trying out her ankle.*

TOM. Saw you run in Munich. One of the great moments of my life. Made one proud. Tears behind the eyes. Must help having something like that to remember.

LACES. Yes.

>*He shouts.*

>Farr, it'll be your own funeral.

MURIEL (*shouting back*). Spoil sport!

TOM. Her injury bad?

LACES. She's seeing the physio this morning.

TOM. I could have wept. Thinking what those girls must feel. Seeing robots taking women's medals. (*Pause.*) What was it like? Standing up there? Seeing the flag go up? Hearing your national anthem!

LACES. I'm a Scot. (*Pause.*) A lot of noise. An awful lot of noise. And I felt very tiny in the middle of it and huge at the same time.

TOM. Two years is a long time to keep a steeple chase record.

LACES. There to be broken.

TOM. The name Laces? Always wondered.

LACES. Trade secret.

>*Enter* VIVIEN.

VIVIEN. Do you never listen to a word?

MURIEL. A few stretches. That's all. Just to see how it feels.

VIVIEN. Well?

MURIEL. It's a bit tight.

PAULINE. The bandages. I told you.

VIVIEN. My strapping?

MURIEL. Yes.

VIVIEN. I've seen it done before now. Whip off the bandage. Do a few strides. Put it back on again and think I won't notice.

MURIEL. I'm not stupid.

VIVIEN. Twenty-four hours without any pressure on it.

MURIEL. I've got a day's teaching to do.

VIVIEN. That's up to you.

MURIEL. I can't not show up.

PAULINE. Stand on the sideline and blow your whistle. Take the pressure off them as well.

MURIEL. You try it.

PAULINE. No thanks. (*She yawns.*) Can I have a word, Dr Blackwood.

VIVIEN. Is it urgent?

PAULINE. I'll probably live.

VIVIEN. If she's insisting on going to school I'd better have a look at her first. You can catch me after that. But had better be snappy. I've got to be at the hospital by 9.30.

PAULINE. Will do. Thanks. (*She runs off.*)

TOM. Those four girls have got a wealth of talent but it needs polishing.

LACES. Any suggestions?

TOM. I'd drop Muriel Farr.

LACES. Why?

TOM. She's not consistent. (*He watches* VIVIEN *and* MURIEL *leave.*) There's a young girl up and coming. Very promising. Janet Morris. People are saying great things.

Enter MIKE. *He starts his recovery.*

Mike Bassett's the sort of lad you should take on. Girls are all very well but — second division stuff. No hope of promotion to the big time. I mean all this Ortolan stuff. How much are you getting from them?

Silence from LACES. MIKE *pants.*

Silence one of the conditions?

LACES. Not the sort of thing you discuss.

TOM. I'm Tom Billbow. I'm not a spy from the three As.

PAULINE comes on.

MIKE. O.K?

PAULINE. Fine. No Dorcas?

MIKE. No.

PAULINE. Drove all the way in this morning. Nearly stalled at a roundabout. Muriel thinks I'll pass next time.

MIKE. Then what?

PAULINE. I'll get one, one day. You'll see. Not a Porsche but something.

Enter HILARY. *Very smart in fur. She looks round.*

I'd kill for a coat like that.

TOM *watches* HILARY. *Pause.* LACES *starts to get ready to go in.*

TOM. You know anything about this film that's supposed to be going on?

LACES. Sorry?

TOM. Film?

LACES. Bottom track.

TOM. Thanks. (TOM *goes.*)

MIKE. One more. (*He runs.*)

LACES. You must have been up with the lark this morning.

HILARY. The early bird catches the worm. I'd like you to make some introductions.

LACES. I've got to take a shower.

HILARY. On your way in. And I want a word.

LACES. Urgent?

HILARY. I think Saturday deserves some explanation. (*They have reached* PAULINE.)

LACES. Pauline, have you met Hilary Davenport?

PAULINE. Hi.

HILARY. Hello, I represent Ortolan.

LACES. I'll be in the changing-room.

HILARY. Right.

LACES *goes.* HILARY *smiles at* PAULINE.
Pause.

HILARY. Are you always out this early?

PAULINE. When we can get the lights.

HILARY. Lights?

PAULINE. Floods. Laces has to be here. They don't call it a proper training session without him.

HILARY. And he's here every morning?

PAULINE. Most.

A pause which is fortunately filled by the entrance of SUE *and* NOËL *going home.*

PAULINE. Have you finished?

SUE. Yes, for this morning.

HILARY. Hello, I'm Hilary Davenport.

PAULINE. From Ortolan.

SUE. Pleased to meet you.

NOËL (*shaking hands*). I'm Sue's Dad.
Pause.

HILARY. All this. You must all be very fit.

The lights go out.

PAULINE. Shit!

SUE. Pauline!

HILARY *looks at her.*

HILARY. It's all right — I don't mind. As long as it's not in public. We do have an image to think of.

NOËL. She understands all that. Don't you love? Not that she does swear, Miss Davenport.

HILARY. I have to find the changing-rooms.

NOËL. I'll show you. (*They go.*)

PAULINE. Well?

SUE. I thought they'd be like the clothing companies. Just send you a list to tick.

They watch her.

PAULINE. What you doing today?

SUE. Not much. You?

PAULINE. Not much.

SUE. Four-thirty tonight?

PAULINE. Yes.

NOËL *comes back.*

NOËL. They're called after the bird. Ortolan. The garden bunting. A migrant. I think it's brown and gold. Never seen one.

You coming?

SUE. Yes. (*They go.*)

PAULINE *continues.* MIKE *runs across the stage.*

Scene Three

The men's changing-room.

> *Enter* HILARY. *She reads* TOM BILLBOW's *column while she
> waits for* LACES *to come out of the shower. Enter* LACES *in
> a towel.*

HILARY. I thought it would smell. Jock straps and all that.
Men's feet are notorious.

LACES. I'm a fresh-socks-every-morning man.

HILARY. I'd guessed that. I'd noticed that next morning women
smell their knickers and men smell their socks. I bet you're the
sort that takes a clean pair with you.

LACES. I've been known to go barefoot. (*He throws his soap and
shampoo beside her.*)

HILARY. I hope the commercial will finally convince you about
the value of our shampoo.

LACES. You don't do a dandruff version.

HILARY. Any problem you don't have.

LACES. I'm sure you'll come up with it for me.

HILARY. I want to know what went wrong yesterday.

LACES. They were outclassed.

HILARY. Why?

LACES. Let's not mull.

HILARY. In my world if a product flops you look for a reason.

Pause.

LACES. The whole of the sporting press is throwing reasons at us.

HILARY. Yes and most of them are words like third-rate and
amateur.

LACES. They *are* amateurs. That's why they need Ortolan to
sponsor them.

HILARY. If they don't win Ortolan doesn't sell.

LACES. You can't buy results in athletics.

HILARY. The weekend we announce the whole sponsorship deal
is hardly the weekend to flop. Our rivals must have been
thrilled. I can hear them laughing. (*Pause*.) We were led to
expect a certain amount of competence.

LACES. They were competent.

HILARY. Only to the degree that no one dropped the baton.
Newton's law of gravitation when applied to a baton not
passed properly I could have explained. But it was the tortoise
and the hare.

LACES. I didn't say anything was certain.

HILARY. Almost. Do you know how much is tied up in that
commercial?

LACES. More than our pittance.

HILARY. You've hardly proved you deserve that.

LACES. You can't expect results overnight.

HILARY. When *can* we expect them? (LACES *shrugs*.) All right.
You and I are in this until Athens. Let's try and get something
out of it. Why don't you sit down and tell me — realistically —
what I can expect?

LACES. I'd like you to see a doctor?

HILARY. I beg your pardon?

LACES. Doctor Vivien Blackwood. Used to be an athlete. In the
early fifties.

HILARY. You trying to pass the buck?

LACES. No. (*He starts to dress.*)

HILARY. Have you ever tried using a sunlamp?

Enter MIKE.

MIKE. Ah —

LACES. Do you know our sponsor?

HILARY. Hello, Hilary Davenport.

MIKE. More post-mortems?

HILARY. In a manner of speaking.

LACES. She's just going.

MIKE. It's O.K. I'll shower at home.

LACES. How's Dorcas?

MIKE. Had the video on all night. Thirty, forty times. Not even the whole two hundred. Just the moment when Sue moves in front.

LACES. Record your own?

MIKE. My start's a bit slow. I was quite pleased with the rest of it.

HILARY. What's the relay like on the video?

MIKE. Sue started very slowly and Muriel went flat out and pulled something coming out of the bend. It was lost before Dorcas got the baton. She runs bloody well when she gets it.

LACES. She coming in?

MIKE *shrugs.*

HILARY. Have you any ideas how we could improve things?

MIKE. You know how it is. They could run the same race today and be terrific.

HILARY. What I ask is a little consistency.

MIKE. They don't get enough time together to be consistent. Ask him.

HILARY. Is that always going to be a problem?

LACES. Not now we've got some money behind us. Before it was a case of taking what we could get. Running whoever was around at the time. No matter if they'd practised together or not. If we couldn't afford to bring Sue down we had to put in a hurdler or someone who was available, but not a sprinter.

MIKE. Dorcas thinks you should pull Sue. Bring in Janet Morris.

HILARY. Who?

LACES. 200 meters runner. Trains with the Cheetahs.

HILARY. She good?

LACES. Very young.

MIKE. She is good.

HILARY. Perhaps you should try her out.

LACES. I am. Lunchtime.

HILARY. I beg your pardon.

LACES. It's called teaching your grandmother to suck eggs.

HILARY. She's got potential?

LACES. I'll tell you when I've seen her. It's a pretty mature team here. She's seventeen, eighteen; there could be all sorts of problems.

HILARY. I'm sure you'll be able to sort them out.

LACES (*to* MIKE). I was going to ask you if you'd like to come down. I could give you half an hour on your start before I see her.

MIKE. Be great.

LACES. Bottom track. 12.30-ish?

MIKE. I'll be there. I've got to get the milk for the muesli.

HILARY. What shampoo do you use?

MIKE. Washing-up liquid. It's cheaper.

HILARY. If you don't mind a product aimed at women, I'll get you a box of Golden Girls.

MIKE. Great. (*He goes.*)

HILARY. I can't have them bringing out Squeezy bottles in front of cameras. How good is this Janet Morris girl?

LACES. There's a lot she could improve.

HILARY *paces.*

HILARY. Enough to add her to the team?

LACES. First you have the attitude, then the physique and the rest you make up on training.

HILARY. How much can she improve?

LACES. They say the most anyone can do is 15%.

HILARY. 15?

LACES. By conventional means. You can push it a bit further with drugs of course. But a woman who looks like a man is hardly going to sell shampoo.

HILARY. We want girls. Real girls. Wholesome.

Legally and decently how are you going to improve them?

LACES. I want a team doctor. Not just running repairs but someone who could really work things out. What they should be eating, when. Just how much more they could improve their oxygen take up. It wouldn't be everyday stuff. But graphs and charts. And their minds. Vivien ran herself. She understands the psychology.

HILARY. I can't see any objection.

LACES. It means more money.

HILARY. More? I know the myth about big organisations is that they can throw money about as they please. But we have shareholders. We are accountable.

Pause.

LACES. You want results. Not results. Records. Medals. To win gold medals you have to come first. That means beating other countries. Behind the iron curtain they test them for athletic potential at five. Then it's special schools, indoor tracks, monitoring. Doctors. Vivien would give us a chance against that. I'm asking you to add her to the list.

HILARY. This woman's good?

LACES. She's ambitious. She knows her stuff.

HILARY. Is she a close friend?

LACES. Vivien's fifteen years older than me.

HILARY. I'm not making any promises.

LACES. She could convince you.

HILARY. We should meet.

LACES. You'll like her. You've got a lot in common. (*Their eyes meet.*)

Scene Four

MIKE *and* DORCAS's *house. Early morning.*

DORCAS *sits on the floor watching the video. She sits in the middle of a shaft of light through the curtains, in front of her on the floor a bowl of muesli. She watches the moment when* SUE *overtakes her several times.*

DORCAS. I know not to say anything before a race. Never speak, not even if they want to shake your hand and wish you luck. Don't let them be there. My head opened in the midde of the race. Cracked. Noise, everything came in. I could feel my spikes going into the track. My feet on the ground. I found myself running wide on the bend. I knew it. Knowing as I did it that I did it. White arms and legs in front of me coming out of the bend.
Scrub it.

Silence. She wipes the tape.

Enter MIKE *with milk and morning paper.*

MIKE. I'm home.

He picks up the bowl of muesli from in front of DORCAS. *He puts milk on it but she won't take it from him.*

MIKE. Paper? (*Silence.*) Tom Billbow isn't pleasant. I thought you could do without me bringing that back. (*Silence.*) At least admit it's today and open the curtains. (*Silence.*) Sometimes I wish I lived with a bus conductress. (*She looks at him.*) I didn't mean it. I'm sorry. (*Pause.*) Sorry. (*Pause.*) Is there nothing I can say? (*Silence.*) I know what it's like. But you have to snap out of it. Forget it. It's over and done. (*Her silence is frightening. Pause.*) You've said that to me enough times. Why can't you do it? Dorcas? (*He tries to give her the bowl.*) The shampoo woman was at the centre. Talking to Laces. He wants to change the squad. He's going to try out Janet Morris. Thought you'd be pleased. (*She remains silent.*) You can't win every time, Dorcas. Even you. The world's not like that. The relay was lost before the baton even got to you. You know that. You can see it on there. When Pauline comes up to you. I can see you know. It's all over your face. Why didn't you just drop the baton? At least it would have been cut and dried. (*Silence*.) I've not got time to talk you out of it. I've got a tutorial at ten. Have you got choir practice tonight?

DORCAS. Yes.

MIKE. You going?

DORCAS. No point. The performance is the same day as the Gateshead meet. Won't be here. Why?

MIKE. We can afford a drink each this evening or the Totem on Friday night?

DORCAS. Totem, on Friday night.

Enter SUE *with two buckets. Silence.*

SUE. Someone's bust the hose to the camper. We can't wash the pots.

MIKE. It's free. Help yourself.

SUE *goes through to the kitchen.*

DORCAS. Why did you tell her she could?

MIKE. It's stupid them trekking back and forth to the centre.

DORCAS. She'll be wanting baths here next. Leaving talcum powder all over our floor.

MIKE. It's pretty rough on Sue.

DORCAS. It's creepy. Living like tramps. Why don't they get a flat.

MIKE. Lots of students live in caravans.

DORCAS. They don't live with their Dads. All that stuff on the way back last night, about how many things he could cook at the same time on one gas ring.

MIKE. Perhaps we ought to ask them for a meal or something.

DORCAS. He'd really love sweet potato!

MIKE. I could do chips or something.

DORCAS. If they want chips there are chip shops.

MIKE. It's tough on Sue.

DORCAS. They don't have to live like that. They could go back up north where they belong.

MIKE. Who'd she have to coach her?

DORCAS. She isn't doing that badly with Noël.

MIKE. He's not that hot.

DORCAS. Yesterday?

MIKE. Fluke and you know it. Laces reckons if he could get her off Noël —

DORCAS. 200.

MIKE. Yes. (DORCAS *goes silent*.) It would make a lot of sense. (DORCAS *is silent*.) All four of you with the same trainer. That's what Ortolan wants.

Enter SUE *with buckets of water*.

SUE. I had to move your things to get the bucket under the tap.

MIKE. That's okay. Would you like a hand?

SUE. I wondered if I could have a look at the video. If it's not a nuisance.

MIKE. We're not watching anything. Dorcas?

SUE. Not if it's any trouble. Just while it was fresh in my mind.

MIKE. I'll just set it up for you.

SUE. Thanks. Have you seen it?

DORCAS is silent.

MIKE. Doesn't Noël want to see it?

SUE. Twenty minutes without him talking tactics in my ear. It's called peace and quiet. O.K?

MIKE. Do you want a cup of tea or anything?

SUE. I'll just have a quick look then go.

MIKE *is puzzled by the fact that the tape seems empty*.

MIKE. Have you changed the tapes?

DORCAS. No.

MIKE. This is empty.

SUE. Dorcas, I'll set it if you can't make out how the timer works.

DORCAS. It's wiped.

SUE. You what?

DORCAS. Wiped. O.K. All gone.

SUE. Why?

DORCAS. I'd seen what I wanted.

SUE. My tape.

DORCAS. Half your tape.

SUE. You couldn't have a video if we didn't put in half.

DORCAS. Who says?

SUE. You were the one who asked us to.

DORCAS. Then don't. We'll be O.K.

SUE. All right.

MIKE. That was a pretty stupid thing to do.

SUE. No one wins all the time Dorcas. It's not like that.

> DORCAS *throws a bucket of water at* SUE. SUE *tries to dry herself.*

> You ought to be reported.

DORCAS. Who to?

SUE. To the W three As.

DORCAS. For what?

MIKE. Do you want a towel?

SUE. It's O.K. I'm sorry about the carpet.

MIKE. I'll fill it up for you.

SUE. It doesn't matter. (*Pause.*) Can i have my bucket. Please? (DORCAS *gives it to her.* SUE *goes.*)

MIKE. You're impossible. Do you know that? (*Pause.*) It'll get round, you know.

DORCAS. I don't care.

MIKE. Don't you want friends?

DORCAS. No.

MIKE. I'll get a cloth

DORCAS *stands.* MIKE *comes back with a cloth.*

If you feel so angry, vent it out there. Run it off. Use it.

DORCAS. You really are beginning to sound like a teacher!

MIKE. If I ever get a kid who behaves like you in a class I'll send them out. Why do you have to act so thick?

DORCAS. Because I'm a stupid black.

MIKE. You're a fantastic athlete.

DORCAS. Because when I was at school they thought I was thick. So they let me spend all my time out on the track. 'At least she's got something to keep her occupied.'

MIKE. If you want qualifications start taking classes. Work.

DORCAS. I have to train.

MIKE. However much you train there's always going to be the way down. And the rest of your life.

DORCAS. I'll quit at the top. A blaze of glory. People will take me very seriously.

MIKE. Eat.

Scene Five

The track. Mid-day.

SOUND TAPE. Golden Girls Commercial Reel 3, Shot 2, Take 1. And Action!

Enter HILARY *and* THE GOLDEN GIRL. *Enter* TOM. THE GOLDEN GIRL *exits.* HILARY *to* TOM. *She has a cup of coffee. Pause.*

TOM. Put a drop in it for you if you like.

HILARY. It's O.K. This place is very organised. They have a place where you can get coffee.

TOM. They're making a commercial for a firm called Ortolan. They're the ones who've just announced the sponsorship deal for the women's relay team. I'm surprised they haven't pulled out after yesterday.

HILARY. What do you know about the women's relay team?

TOM. On paper they're potential champions. But yesterday was a bloody disgrace. Do you follow athletics?

HILARY. A little.

TOM. They're a national team we could have pride in. Don't you think?

HILARY *nods.*

A sort of identifying process. About the only time you hear the national anthem now. Sports events. The Germans' ll think they're invincible now they're down to forty-one seconds.

HILARY. Records are there to be broken.

TOM. Sure I can't put a drop in there for you?

HILARY. Quite sure. I'm interested. Go on.

TOM. As individuals they're wonderful.

HILARY. As a team?

TOM. They need time together.

HILARY. You sound like a coach.

TOM. Used to do a bit of javelin throwing. I mean — you wouldn't think it now. But I did. Do you know anything about the javelin?

HILARY. Nothing.

TOM. Ruined by the use of steroids. You cheated or you lost or you quit. I'm not a good loser.

HILARY. You were offered drugs?

TOM. They were going to be a miracle. Then they started dope testing and a lot of competitiors declined to take part. There are world champions who are confined to wheelchairs. They didn't realise if they took too much their bones would go.

HILARY. And now?

TOM. They find out somebody's using something — they ban it. Find something else that's harder to detect.

SOUND TAPE. Can we reposition the logo on the running vest?

TOM. The point will come when the drugs are so sophisticated that the tests will become too expensive. The people putting the money in will refuse to pay for them.

SOUND TAPE. Miss Davenport —

TOM. They'll go like the notion of the amateur.

SOUND TAPE. Miss Davenport!

HILARY. Excuse me. I'm wanted.

TOM. Thought you didn't look like an athlete. You use it?

HILARY. Pardon?

TOM. This new shampoo. I wondered if you ever used it?

HILARY. Yes, actually.

TOM. It looks very nice. Your hair.

HILARY. Thank you.

She goes. TOM *watches her. Enter* MIKE *and* LACES. MIKE *with blocks.*

LACES. Try moving them over. (MIKE *does this*.) Not that much. Just a fraction. There!

MIKE. Down?

LACES. Yes O.K. I'll give you the commands and just come up slowly.

Enter NOËL.

NOËL. Mind if I watch?

LACES. Fine by me.

MIKE. No problem.

LACES. One, two three —

MIKE *comes up off the blocks.* THE GOLDEN GIRL *runs across.* MIKE *stops in his tracks. He looks round.* NOËL *and* LACES, *intent on* MIKE, *have not noticed.*

LACES. You could do me the credit of concentrating.

NOËL. His head's too high.

MIKE. Did you —

LACES. It's not in alignment.

SOUND TAPE. Cut!

LACES. Mike!

MIKE. Sorry. (MIKE *walks back and gets on his marks again.*)

LACES. Is that comfortable?

MIKE. Feels O.K.

LACES. Is it comfortable?

MIKE. Start I always use.

LACES *adjusts* MIKE's *head.*

LACES. Feel better?

MIKE. It's going into my shoulders.

LACES. Relax.

MIKE *gets up and shakes himself out.*

NOËL. Have you tried moving his hands forward?

MIKE. I've been through all that.

LACES *has a feel up* MIKE's *spine.*

NOËL. When was the last time you saw a physio?

MIKE. A couple of weeks.

LACES *indicates to* NOËL *to feel* MIKE's *spine.*

NOËL. A few knots.

LACES. He say anything?

MIKE *shakes his head.* LACES *begins to massage it for him.*

LACES. One lap.

NOËL. Loosener? (*They go.*)

Enter TOM. THE GOLDEN GIRL *runs across. Enter* DORCAS.

DORCAS. Is she supposed to be an athlete?

TOM. Apparently.

DORCAS. She's over-striding.

TOM. Shame they can't use Sue Kinder isn't it?

DORCAS. She's not the only one in the squad.

TOM. Bad feeling in the team is there? Personality clashes? Tiffs over boyfriends?

DORCAS. Who do you think you are?

TOM. Did a bit of athletics myself at one time. I know what it's like. There are rumours about you and Mike Bassett. Things not being easy.

DORCAS. Mike's irrelevant.

TOM. Do me a favour?

DORCAS. What?

TOM. I'd like your autograph.

(*She laughs.*)

I believe in you.

HILARY *comes back.*

HILARY. Dorcas . . . Hilary Davenport. I'm responsible for Ortolan's sponsorship.

TOM. Give her the money. Whatever she wants. She'll be worth it. Every penny. She'll get it back for you. (TOM *goes.*)

HILARY. Is that man drunk?

DORCAS. He's from the papers.

Enter THE GOLDEN GIRL.

HILARY. Well done. You must have seen our adverts. This is Anna, our Golden Girl.

DORCAS. If you stand up, you'll breathe better.

THE GOLDEN GIRL. My last job was in a jacuzzi!

HILARY. This is Dorcas Ableman.

THE GOLDEN GIRL. I feel silly. I wish I had your dedication.

DORCAS. I wish I had your money.

SOUND TAPE. Sorry, we have to do it again. Thank you, Anna.

THE GOLDEN GIRL. *Ciao!* (ANNA *and* HILARY *go*.)

   Re-enter MIKE, NOËL *and* LACES.

MIKE. Janet Morris.

JANET (*off*). Track!

LACES. She's supposed to report to me!

   They watch. LACES *starts his stopwatch. They say nothing for 23 seconds. Something extraordinary is obviously going on.* LACES *stops the clock.*

LACES. I don't believe it! Hardly accurate from this distance.

NOËL. You thinking of bringing her into the squad?

LACES. It's crossed my mind.

NOËL. And drop who?

LACES. She's still very young.

NOËL. Tell you who she should go in for.

LACES. If I need your advice on my squad, I'll ask. (*Pause.*) She's never run in an international.

NOËL. She's done 22.18.

LACES. Not officially.

   HILARY *to* LACES.

HILARY. Is that her?

LACES. Yes.

HILARY. She's black.

LACES. Sorry?

HILARY. You didn't say she wasn't white. I sort of assumed —

LACES. Does it matter?

HILARY. Is she special?

LACES. I want to know what goes on in her head. (*To* DORCAS.) Oi! Where were you this morning?

NOËL. I used to tell my Sue she'd make a film star. I always kept her nice. A real little girl, little girl. It used to surprise people. More than coping with what I did.

HILARY. Your daughter is a great runner.

NOËL. She's not at her best. Not yet. Is she?

LACES. Sorry?

NOËL. Sue. Not at her best. Not yet.

LACES. Probably not.

NOËL. Next year. Have her at her peak for Athens.

SOUND TAPE. That's it for today.

HILARY (*to* LACES). We'll speak soon?

LACES. My pleasure.

HILARY. I'll be in touch.

She goes.

NOËL. The power behind the throne?

LACES. You don't bite the hand that feeds you —

NOËL. Miss Davenport — (NOËL *goes after* HILARY.)

MIKE. I thought Pauline was more your sort.

LACES. Leave it out.

MIKE. It was a very strange sequence you dropped people off in last night.

LACES. Let's talk about Janet Morris.

MIKE. Star of Muriel's school. You should ask Muriel.

Enter JANET MORRIS.

JANET. Mr Mackenzie?

LACES. Yes. And Mike Bassett. Not as glamorous as he looks in the running mags, I'm afraid.

JANET. Hi!

MIKE. Congratulations.

JANET. What?

MIKE. Just now. You were pretty impressive.

JANET. You were watching?

MIKE. Sure.

JANET. Mrs Farr tells me off for it.

LACES. Quite right. You aren't doing yourself any sort of favour by showing off.

JANET. Just a bit of fun.

LACES. I'm not interested in fun.

JANET. Then what's the point?

LACES. I don't like messing.

JANET. I don't mess.

LACES. I'd like to have a look at you with weights. When you're ready. (LACES *goes*.)

MIKE. His bark's worse than his bite.

JANET. He's a Scot. (JANET *blows a raspberry*.)

MIKE. Don't let him hear you do that.

Pause.

JANET. I never thought I'd meet you —

MIKE. You'll get over it.

JANET. You were my pin-up when you took the Commonwealth record. I ran away from — from — somewhere I was staying. All I took, your picture and my running things. In the end it got ripped down by a guy I went with. Mike Bassett — white trash — he didn't let me explain it was to do with your running.

MIKE. You'd better see Laces. (JANET *questions*.) Mr Mackenzie.

JANET. The Scots don't half have weird names. Excuse me, I've some strides to do. Then I'll see him.

MIKE. He doesn't like being messed about with.

JANET. Tell him I'm just finishing.

MIKE. O.K. (*He goes.*)

   JANET *watches him go.* DORCAS *to her.*

DORCAS. Mike giving you advice?

JANET. He's kind, isn't he?

DORCAS. Mike? You're having a trial for the Golden Girls
   Squad?

JANET. Yes.

DORCAS. D'you want to be one of us?

JANET. My dream. I want to go horse-back riding. The stuff for
   that costs a fortune. Have you ever been riding?

DORCAS. I hate horses.

JANET. What do you have to say. To get in?

DORCAS. The more you keep your mouth shut, the better they
   like you. Just show Laces what you can do. That you're
   serious. (*Pause.*) You'll do it.

JANET. You really think so?

DORCAS. You're very, very good.

JANET. Mrs Farr says I'm better than she was when she was my
   age. At school I can beat all the boys. It's their own fault.
   They don't train. I've got to finish.

DORCAS. See you at the next squad session. (JANET *starts off.*)
   Hasten slowly young one. (JANET *stops.*)

JANET. Sorry?

DORCAS. Hasten slowly.

JANET. I don't know what it means.

DORCAS. Don't go too far too fast.

   Pause.

   It's not meant to sound frightening. (DORCAS *goes.*)

JANET. I wanted to be sent away and made to train. When I was a kid I used to whip comics and they had stories of school teams that got kidnapped and forced to train. Baddies wanting them to win because of enormous bets. They grumbled and then escaped. I wanted someone to take me away and tell me I couldn't have chocolates ever again. We got those black pumps for school — the sort with brown bottoms and elastic across the front of your feet. Fitted about four times and then the elastic went all crinkly, fell off your feet all the time. They gave the lads football boots. Because you couldn't be a boy without them. They made me beg to get a proper pair of spikes. Then they were surprised I ran away.

Scene Six

Start in blackout. The multi-gym.

PAULINE, JANET *and* DORCAS *warming up to begin a session* LACES *and* VIVIEN *with clip boards. Enter* SUE *with an empty specimen jar.*

VIVIEN. I want a urine sample in that jar. Try thinking about water. Turn all the taps on and leave the door open.

PAULINE. She doesn't know what running water is.

SUE. We aren't tramps. (SUE *goes.*)

LACES. Oi!

VIVIEN. How much have you got on there? (*She counts it up.*)

JANET. I can do it!

VIVIEN. If you're not careful it will do you. Up. (VIVIEN *adjusts the weights.*) You do nothing until we've worked you out a proper programme.

JANET. Mike Bassett can do it.

VIVIEN. One he's a chap and two he's probably been using weights regularly for the past 10 years.

LACES. What are you doing tonight?

PAULINE. Weights.

LACES. Later?

PAULINE. I'm not interested.

LACES. No one?

PAULINE. Why? Should there be?

LACES. You're attractive.

PAULINE. So?

LACES. I don't understand.

PAULINE. It's not a sacrifice. I don't punish myself.

Enter MURIEL.

MURIEL. Some moron's left all the taps on.

VIVIEN. Most athletes have a sense of timing built into them. Or doesn't yours apply to clocks like the rest of us?

MURIEL. Sorry. George's birthday tomorrow. I had to wait for the cake to be cold enough to put in the tin.

VIVIEN. George or Ortolan. If you're going to take what they're giving, you'd better make sure of what they're getting in return. I want a urine sample in there. I'm not looking for drugs so you can let rip and do a decent amount.

Enter SUE. MURIEL *goes.*

SUE. I couldn't manage any more. Honestly.

VIVIEN. There's a label for it over there. What was Muriel's passing like yesterday.

LACES. Pauline had to move her mark back a bit. Could just be that she's been out of training.

VIVIEN. I can't find anything. Nothing looks wrong when she's moving. She said anything to you?

LACES. I think it's just that she's frightened of doing it again. She say anything to you when you're driving?

PAULINE. Turn right, turn left, stop grinding the gears.

LACES. After that?

PAULINE. You don't have intimate conversations in a 2CV.

VIVIEN. Nothing about how she feels?

PAULINE. If she doesn't do it in Athens, she'll never do it. She knows that.

JANET. You know what they call her at school?

SUE. What?

JANET. Farr-t.

LACES. That's terrible.

DORCAS. Better than being called Wog.

JANET. They've got a new one now.

PAULINE. What?

DORCAS. What?

Pause.

LACES. She'll find out soon enough.

Enter MURIEL.

DORCAS. Did you know you'd got a new nick name?

MURIEL. No.

JANET. Honestly, I wasn't going to tell them Mrs Farr.

MURIEL. What is it?

JANET (*flatly*). So near, but yet so Farr. It's because you always come second. It was the boys that made it up.

VIVIEN. If you want my help in furthering your athletic prowess, perhaps we can get on.

Silence.

One, anybody who has an appointment with me and doesn't keep that appointment without some very good reason isn't going to get very much of my attention. Two, you might not like some of the things you're going to be asked to do but they are in your own interests. I'm not here to turn your bodies into machines, just to make sure that they function at maximum possible efficiency. This afternoon is going to be a list of questions and then an intensive workout to see what you can and can't do. From that we'll work out an interim training schedule to keep you going until the scientific data's been programmed.

DORCAS. I thought we weren't being machines.

VIVIEN. I'm the one that Ortolan pays to be clever. I have just given you a series of forms which are to be filled in every day. Every single day with the number of hours slept and your weight before breakfast . . .

JANET. Excuse me.

VIVIEN. Yes.

JANET. We haven't got no scales.

VIVIEN. Buy some.

JANET. I haven't got any money yet.

LACES. Miss Davenport is coming in this afternoon, she'll sort all that out for you.

VIVIEN. On the other one you write down everything you eat. Not just meals but all the bits and bobs in between as well. Anybody who has sugar in her tea or coffee I want to know how many. The other important thing is exactly how much liquid you're taking in each day. Drinks go on the blue sheet.

SUE. We have a lot of soup. Where does soup go?

VIVIEN. With food but it would be a good idea if you put how much.

DORCAS. How much food as well?

PAULINE. Soup, you idiot.

VIVIEN. The charts are quite self-explanatory once you get the hang of them. Any problems ask me or ask Laces.

DORCAS. How long has this got to go on for?

VIVIEN. Long enough for us to see some overall pattern.

JANET. This is worse than the form I had to get for my passport, Mrs Farr had to help me get that filled in.

MURIEL. This really is rather complicated.

VIVIEN. Is there anyone here who understands it?

One by one they shake their heads.

VIVIEN. Laces and I thought it was —

LACES. Viv, why don't you take them through it?

VIVIEN. Right sit down. I've got time to go through it once so listen. (*To* DORCAS.) How much sleep did you have last night?

DORCAS. Don't know.

VIVIEN. You must have some idea what time you went to bed and what time you got up?

PAULINE. Too much bed, not enough sleep.

DORCAS. Oh, fuck off!

VIVIEN. It doesn't have to be down to the hundredth of a second.

DORCAS. About six hours.

VIVIEN. That all?

DORCAS. I don't need much sleep.

VIVIEN. You put six hours in the column marked Sunday night and so on throughout the week.

SUE. What if you have a sleep during the day?

Pause.

VIVIEN. It had better go in the total for that night.
Food. What did you have for breakfast?

JANET. Toast and tea.

VIVIEN. That's not a very well balanced breakfast.

JANET. I have to have whatever Aunty cooks.

VIVIEN. What about protein? Meat, cheese, fish?

JANET. I don't like cheese.

VIVIEN. What about the others?

JANET. They cost a fortune.

MURIEL. When you get some money —

JANET. Got some bacon. Put it in the fridge and Warren ate it all.

VIVIEN. What about the rest of you?

PAULINE. I'm a vegetarian.

VIVIEN. Yes, you would be.

SUE. How come you've got a leather skirt?

PAULINE. It's the idea of dead flesh. Skin's another matter.

LACES. A bit of hush.

VIVIEN. Where it says Monday breakfast you write down toast.

JANET. Ta.

VIVIEN. You put the cups of tea on the other sheet and so on
    for the rest of the day. The incidentals, chocolate bars, any of
    that rubbish go at the bottom of the column for that day's food.

PAULINE. What's this sheet?

VIVIEN. A few personal details. I'll come to them in a minute.

PAULINE. It's the sort of stuff that ought to go in your diary.

SUE. Only if you've got a diary with a lock.

    Enter NOËL. *He has come to return* LACES' *stopwatch.*

VIVIEN. Do you want something?

NOËL. Is all this weights stuff really necessary?

LACES. As far as I'm concerned.

NOËL. Only I've been reading some stuff and it worries me a bit.

LACES. Noël, this isn't really the time or the place.

VIVIEN. Mr Kinder, I'm expected to help these girls get results.
    I have to do that on my own.

NOËL. I won't interfere.

LACES. Please, just go away.

SUE. This is Ortolan stuff Dad. They pay for it. Go on. I'll tell
    you all about it later.

NOËL. Right. (NOËL *gives* LACES *the stopwatch. He goes*.)

SUE. He used to be the only Dad at sports day. He went berserk when I lost the egg and spoon race. Who's going to see this?

DORCAS. Something you don't want your Dad to know about?

VIVIEN. It's strictly confidential between me and Laces.

SUE. Laces, I just don't think we should be asked these questions.

LACES. Vivien's territory, not mine.

SUE. They've got nothing to do with the way we run.

DORCAS (*to* MURIEL). Miss Prim and Proper.

VIVIEN. I beg your pardon but the scientific data would disagree. There wouldn't be scientific data if other girls hadn't answered the same questions.

DORCAS. It's only when you're on, what sort of precautions you take.

VIVIEN. I'm not prepared to put you on continual cycles of the pill so menstruation doesn't interfere with your training, unless they're answered. If you're embarassed because there's a man in the room I'll ask him to leave.

SUE. Are we having an internal examination as well?

VIVIEN. You will do.

JANET. What examinations?

DORCAS. They poke your insides about.

PAULINE. Abortions?

VIVIEN. If any of you get as good as you want to be, that skeleton will probably come rattling out of the cupboard along with a lot of others.

PAULINE. What's it got to do with Ortolan?

MURIEL. Bloody firm. Your body's not your own.

DORCAS. Do you want a list of who, where, when as well?

VIVIEN. Not at this stage. The more details we have —

DORCAS. You don't need this much.

PAULINE. I . . . .

VIVIEN. Perhaps you'll allow me to be the expert.

DORCAS. Ortolan doesn't own us!

LACES. I'm sure in your case Dorcas they'll be very glad to know that.

VIVIEN. I suggest you take these home and decide just how important you think winning is. You all know how to take your own pulse? (*Yes from all of them.*) Does anyone have any objection to having her pulse rate recorded?

(*Nothing from the girls.*) This week before every session, and before means before warm-ups as well, I want you to take your resting pulse rate and record that. Your rate again after maximum effort. Again 5 minutes later. Laces if you'd like to count us through thirty seconds. Then your usual warm up and on to the weights when you're ready.

LACES. O.K. Starting now —

They start taking their pulses.

Enter HILARY.

HILARY. Good news about —

LACES. Shush.

HILARY. Sorry. Everything O.K.?

LACES *nods.*

LACES. And stop. (*The girls work out the results.*) They're just about to start a new session.

HILARY. A quick word that's all. I have to get back to London tonight.

VIVIEN. If it is a quick word. Locums become expensive at night.

HILARY. You're very conscientious about our money.

VIVIEN. Wasn't I expected to be?

JANET (*to* LACES). Will you ask her about my money?

VIVIEN (*to* SUE). Try getting absolutely straight there. That's it.

HILARY (*to* LACES). Is there a problem with money?

LACES. She hasn't got her golden card yet.

HILARY. I've been trying to chase it up for her. Legally she's a minor, big stores won't give them credit. It's very difficult.

LACES. You must have some clout with them.

HILARY. I'm afraid it's going to have to be receipts until your birthday.

LACES. Next month.

DORCAS. Hard luck, Morris Minor.

HILARY. There can't be anything you want that badly. Let me know if there is.

VIVIEN. I can't delay the session for you.

HILARY. Sorry. Is it O.K. if I talk to them while they're doing . . .

LACES. They're quite *compos mentis.*

VIVIEN *claps her hands twice.*

VIVIEN. Come on, sit down.

HILARY. I'd like to spend a few minutes with you on the do's and don'ts of being the Golden Girls squad. We don't believe that sponsors should interfere with their er — there's not really a word for it — those we're sponsoring. But if you work for any organisation there are a few ground rules. I've brought with me several crates of Golden Girls shampoo and from now on I'd ask you only to use Golden Girls. I've brought up your tracksuits and running togs. I know yellow doesn't suit everybody —

SUE. I look dreadful in yellow.

HILARY. But I think our designers have managed to find a shade that will do justice to all of you. We're keen for you to wear these at all times. I know that some of you have certain affinities to various articles of clothing but I hope you'll be able to re-invest those in the Golden Girls kit. No one wants to lay down rules of behaviour to grown women but I think you must all realise that being a Golden Girl has certain responsibilities. Obviously we want winners but if you don't win, don't forget the glory there is to be obtained by being a

good loser. The joy of the race is in the running, after all. I
think we'd all agree that we wouldn't look up to a heroine
who swears like a trooper, even if she has just lost. I needn't
stress how important it is for you to stress that you are
sponsored by us. That as athletes you are assisted by us for the
money that allows you to compete and a little that we put
into your trust funds but nothing more. No one wants to hear
the dirty rustle of five pound notes.

PAULINE. I wouldn't mind, however dirty.

HILARY *allows herself to laugh.*

HILARY. Have I missed out anything Laces?

LACES. Sounds fine to me.

HILARY. One more thing. Any trouble, any sort of suspension
or ban and we'll drop you like a hot potato.

DORCAS. Can we drop you if you do something we don't like?

HILARY. What could we possibly do?

SUE. Don't you test shampoo on the eyes of rabbits, things like
that?

HILARY. The last thing I want to say is you'll find it difficult in
interviews — people will do everything they can to avoid you
mentioning the name of the product. But the more accidental
slips you make the more you help our sales and consequently
what we can invest in you. It can become a little game. We're
going to reward you with an extra £100 in your trust funds
everytime you manage to mention Ortolan or Golden Girls.
Most of all I want you to enjoy the benefits that Ortolan's
sponsorship can give you and to put everything you can
towards first Gateshead and Crystal Palace and then triumphing
in Athens. Do that and we'll see where we can go from there.

Silence.

JANET. Thank you.

HILARY. I think Dr Blackwood wants to get on. I'll explain to
Laces about your money.

JANET. Ta.

HILARY. Will you take me out for tea?

LACES. I thought you were in a hurry?

HILARY. I've got half an hour. Or I could take you. It's all Ortolan's money after all.

VIVIEN. I can manage here if Miss Davenport wants a word.

LACES. I'd just like to check the weights. (*He does.*)

MURIEL. How many are we doing?

VIVIEN. I want it all out. Everything you've got. The moment it starts being unendurable stop. And . . .

HILARY. How's it going?

VIVIEN. You don't know until the clock stops.

HILARY. You ran yourself?

VIVIEN. Yes.

HILARY. Why?

VIVIEN. Pleasure.

HILARY. I find it quite extraordinary.

VIVIEN. Wanting to be good at something? You must understand ambition.

HILARY *smiles.*

HILARY. What do you get out of this?

VIVIEN. The chance to do some pure research. There's a chair in medical psychology coming up in about three years time that I'd like to go for.

HILARY. Is that enough time to make a reputation?

VIVIEN. I know a lot about timing my run from the back.

Pause.

HILARY. I want golden girls.

VIVIEN. I'll give them to you.

LACES. Right, they're all set. I'll do the tea. You don't look as if you'll cost me gateau.

HILARY. I might surprise you.

They go.

VIVIEN. I want it all out. Everything you've got.

The girls start to work seriously. It becomes more and more powerful. VIVIEN watches in a white coat. When you think it's about to become unendurable the lights blackout.

Scene Seven

VIVIEN'S *room*

Enter LACES. *He prys. Enter* VIVIEN.

VIVIEN. Sorry, I seem to have a locum for the locum.

LACES. I managed to amuse myself.

VIVIEN. They're supposed to be private and confidential.

LACES. You get to know a lot about them, their ups, their downs.

VIVIEN. Dorcas?

LACES. I'm getting there.

VIVIEN. You'll be glad to know a lot of it's better than I expected. On paper the way Janet eats looks like malnutrition. Sue's quite anaemic but that's easy enough to sort out. A few vitamin supplements all round wouldn't really go amiss.

LACES. What about getting them to change their diets?

VIVIEN. I'm not giving cooking lessons.

Pause.

There's something I want to try. Don't look suspicious before you've heard me out.

LACES. It's something you don't think I'm going to like.

VIVIEN. Just hear me out.

LACES. If it's not legal I don't want to know.

VIVIEN. It wouldn't show up in urine tests.

LACES. Blood tests?

VIVIEN. Nowhere.

LACES. Not a drug?

VIVIEN. A drug that no one would ever be able to prove.

LACES. Then it's not ethical.

VIVIEN. You can't be a purist. Sport isn't like that any more.

LACES. An unfair advantage?

VIVIEN. Against whom? The Germans? They'd take anything
that would give them an advantage against the Lynikova's of
this world, if they knew it was safe.

LACES. There isn't anything safe.

VIVIEN. This is.

LACES. They know everything legitimate that's on the market.

VIVIEN. But this is brand new. Hydromel.

LACES. Doesn't Hydromel show up?

VIVIEN. Not if they aren't really taking it. Not if they're really
taking something else.

LACES. A placebo?

VIVIEN. Exactly. There's a pill called Similexon. It's made from
sugar and cornstarch. The stuff turkish delight is rolled in. But
they'll think it's Hydromel. They'd think it gave them a
fighting chance. If there was any other way I could give them
self-belief.

LACES. It's still cheating.

VIVIEN. You'd have no objection to them training at altitude?

LACES. They'd still have scruples.

VIVIEN. Well Dorcas doesn't have them for a start.

LACES. She's asked?

VIVIEN. Not in as many words. Questions about other teams.
What are they on. Where do they get it? Why aren't they

found out.

LACES. Well hardly —

VIVIEN. If other athletes are prepared to take something to win, so is she.

LACES. That's Dorcas, the others?

VIVIEN. Sue would do whatever was necessary to keep up with Dorcas and so on.

LACES. I'm not convinced.

VIVIEN. See this?

LACES. Urine analysis?

VIVIEN. My urine after taking Similexon. Can you see anything that shows?

LACES. No.

VIVIEN. Precisely. There is nothing. But they might — and I'm not saying it's a certainty — they might find themselves a couple of hundredths of a second.

LACES. If they were found?

VIVIEN. There's nothing to find. Think of the future it would give them. I'm a doctor. Trust me.

Scene Eight

The women's locker room.

MURIEL, DORCAS, SUE *and* PAULINE. MURIEL *has made* JANET *a birthday cake.*

MURIEL. Have you got the candles?

DORCAS. No. I've got something else. (DORCAS *takes a toy car from her locker.*)

MURIEL. What?

PAULINE. She's coming. Quick!

MURIEL. What's that?

DORCAS. It's a Morris Minor for Morris Minor.

Enter JANET. *She has just been on her first Ortolan shopping trip and she's bought meat, bathroom scales and running shoes. The others sing her happy birthday.*

MURIEL. You'd better take it off, so we don't have to put Morris Minor down on the diet sheets.

DORCAS. Wish.

JANET *shuts her eyes, wishes and blows.*

SUE. Bet I know what you wished.

JANET. What?

SUE. I know.

JANET. You can't know.

DORCAS. Something about Gateshead?

JANET *is embarassed.*

PAULINE. Presents?

JANET. Stuff we had to buy with our money.

MURIEL *is slicing the cake and handing it round.*

MURIEL. No one's mentioning this, O.K? Or you don't get a slice.

SUE. O.K.

MURIEL. Happy Birthday.

DORCAS. Morris Minor.

JANET. I'm a Morris Major now. (JANET *gets out the scales.*)

MURIEL. That furry stuff'll just get matted.

JANET. I thought they'd be warm. (*She stands on them and watches the dial while she eats her cake.*)

DORCAS. You got your gold card then?

JANET. Yes. It's exciting, isn't it? Just getting things not having to give people any money. This isn't making any difference.

SUE. Did you get anything exciting?

JANET. Four pairs of spikes. And meat. This huge piece of steak. Bigger than the T-bones you get at the Totem.

DORCAS. Is it O.K. for you to come with us tonight?

JANET. Aunty says I'm legally old enough to come home drunk.

PAULINE. And?

JANET. And what?

PAULINE. Other things.

JANET. I didn't need anything else. They had some nice jeans.

SUE. Why didn't you get them?

JANET. They get you jeans?

PAULINE. Why not? They don't want you to go round looking like a frump.

DORCAS. If you like you can come in with us.

MURIEL. She's too young to want all those things.

DORCAS. We have a little system. If there's something one of us really wants, we all go down to Pearts and pool our credit.

DORCAS. That's how we got the settee.

JANET. I thought it had to be to do with running?

DORCAS. I like to put my feet up after a hard day on the track.

SUE. You should have got yourself something new for tonight.

JANET. I didn't know.

> DORCAS *goes to open her locker.*

DORCAS. Like it?

JANET. Great. Mike'll really like it. He likes blue.

> *Pause.*

MURIEL. Front room curtains. (*She takes yards of curtain fabric from her locker.*) I'm going to do them with a triple pleat at the top. And this is for the back bedroom. (*More fabric.*)

> SUE *takes a water carrier with a tap from her locker.*

SUE. For Dad. So he doesn't go on moaning about the one we've got. Have you seen this dress?

JANET *is dazed; she stands on the scales.*

PAULINE (*bringing out a fur coat*). It mightn't be quite Hilary Davenport but — (*The room is strewn with goodies.*)

JANET. I just brought my best jeans.

MURIEL. Put yours on, Dorcas.

DORCAS. Only if you are.

MURIEL. Sue?

They start to get dressed up.

PAULINE. Haven't seen your Dad this week?

SUE. He's trying to fix the move.

MURIEL. Here?

SUE. Where else.

DORCAS. What's he going to do?

SUE. Coach.

DORCAS. I thought you were training with Laces now.

SUE. Only while Dad's away.

PAULINE. He'll never get a part-time job here because there aren't any.

SUE. Dole here or dole there, what's the difference?

MURIEL. Hardly worth buying all that stuff.

SUE. Takes ages to sell houses now at home.

PAULINE *begins to decant some other shampoo into a Golden Girls bottle.*

DORCAS. Oi! What're you doing?

PAULINE. I just don't trust Golden Girls, mine gets ever so greasy using it all the time.

She decants shampoo.

JANET. It's cheating.

PAULINE. Who's to know what's inside. (PAULINE *starts to dress up*.)

An alarm goes off in JANET's *bag*. JANET *rushes to get out her Similexon*.

JANET. Why she couldn't give us ones you have to have with your dinner, not 2 hours after. I keep forgetting. Then I get scared I might have to take two on the same day.

MURIEL. Never, ever. Do you hear me?

JANET. Why not?

PAULINE. Because the dose is one. If two were safe she'd give us two.

SUE. Don't you ever think it's cheating?

DORCAS. A fighting chance.

They are nearly dressed.

DORCAS. Have you got any blusher?

PAULINE. In my bag.

JANET. It really suits you, Dorcas.

DORCAS. Thanks. Do you want to borrow something for tonight? Why don't you try this.

JANET. Ta.

MURIEL. Make you the belle of the ball.

She helps JANET *get changed into* DORCAS's *new frock*.

I hear you've been upsetting Mr Dimond?

JANET. He's a wally Mrs Farr — Muriel — he is honestly.

SUE. What size shoes?

JANET. Six.

PAULINE. You can have these, not the most glamorous but —

Enter HILARY.

HILARY. A party, well, well, well.

JANET. Would you like a piece of cake?

HILARY. I thought this sort of thing was strictly forbidden. Well a little fling. I won't say anything. It's Sue I wanted actually. About this weekend.

SUE. It has to be no.

HILARY. For me?

SUE. One weekend. One weekend on my own.

HILARY. That's hardly the way champions talk.

SUE. It's not a competition.

HILARY. We'll fix everything. There and back, everything.

SUE. Two weeks before Gateshead, it's crazy.

HILARY. No pressure. They just want you to put in an appearance and sign a few autographs. It's quite safe.

SUE. I have to run?

HILARY. People will come to see you run.

SUE. No.

HILARY. There's no risk.

PAULINE. She's got a hamstring problem.

HILARY. Are you saying you know what's best for her.

PAULINE. Some things you can do that are silly.

HILARY. Any strains of any sort I'll get the best physio money can buy. You can take it gently.

SUE. I can't run and take it gently.

DORCAS. We've been working towards Gateshead for a long time.

HILARY. Girls. Don't you think you owe Ortolan a favour. I like to think you understand my position. I have to be accountable. Men in suits and waistcoats. All right, Sue. Come on; I'm sure we can come to some arrangement.

SUE. What?

HILARY. Whatever's reasonable.

SUE. Money?

HILARY. Obviously.

Enter LACES.

What about the practice?

LACES. Practice?

HILARY. If she did the Golden Girls promotion in Manchester?

LACES. You haven't got the first idea. You train very carefully to peak for a race. O.K. she goes to Manchester this weekend and then she loses at Gateshead. Is that fine by you?

HILARY. Do you know how much we've got tied up in this promotion?

LACES. I don't care.

HILARY. If we pull out now —

LACES. Everything you've done so far hinges on four girls and forty-one seconds. It's like floating a needle on water. The tiniest slip and it sinks.

HILARY. Listen to me Sue —

LACES. She's said no.

HILARY. Let's just discuss this in a rational manner. What about you Pauline?

LACES. This weekend is off.

HILARY. It's fixed.

LACES. Unfix it.

HILARY. Your whistles, your stopwatches —

LACES. Have them. (LACES *starts to undress.*)

HILARY. Put them on. I'll find another girl.

LACES. My training schedule's full.

HILARY. I believe Mr Kinder wants to do more coaching.

Pause.

LACES. You all look very good. Big night out?

PAULINE. Janet's birthday. We're going to the Totem. Want to come?

HILARY. Don't you dare let me hear of any of you getting drunk. (HILARY *goes*.)

Pause.

SUE. Thanks.

LACES. Did your Dad want you to do it?

SUE. I didn't ask him.

DORCAS. Go on Laces. Come tonight. Please.

LACES. I'll see. Dorcas, I'd like a word. On your own.

DORCAS. What?

LACES. I'm dropping you for Gateshead.

DORCAS. What?

LACES. You, Sue or Janet and I can only take two.

DORCAS. Drop Sue?

LACES. She's been very consistent in training.

DORCAS. I haven't?

LACES. I have to see what Janet can do.

DORCAS. The reserve.

LACES. If something goes wrong I can't bring her in with no experience. Well can I? You want her to have her chance don't you?

DORCAS. Sue. She hates running the relay. Hates it.

LACES. I thought you'd understand.

DORCAS. My place.

LACES. I'm sorry. It's my only option. The start of the season you expect a bit of chopping and changing.

JANET. What about this, Dorcas?

DORCAS *looks at her*.

DORCAS. Athens?

LACES. The best team I can get at the time.

DORCAS. It's that woman that's behind this isn't it?

LACES. No.

DORCAS. My place.

LACES. She's young. A lot of potential. She deserves her chance, Dorcas.

DORCAS. Not my place.

LACES. Then I'm sorry but you won't be running at Gateshead.

DORCAS. I should have been singing. (*She goes.*)

LACES. I'll see you all on the track tomorrow morning. I want to do some more work on the passing. Sue to Pauline and Muriel to Janet.

JANET. What about Dorcas?

LACES. I'm working the team I want to run at Gateshead.

PAULINE. What about tonight?

LACES. I'm sorry. (*He goes.*)

JANET. I'm running at Gateshead?

MURIEL. Looks like it.

JANET. It's what I wished!

PAULINE. Did you wish you'd win?

Scene Nine

The multi-gym

Sound of fast and furious working. Lights. DORCAS is driving herself fanatically. Enter HILARY in pink with a radio.

HILARY. It's O.K. I'm not chasing your place. Business lunches. Alcohol. You begin to understand why men get paunchy. Gateshead. I just couldn't face the drive. I thought you'd be up there supporting Mike Bassett.

DORCAS. Things to do here.

HILARY *starts to warm up: an imitation of the athletes.* DORCAS *works properly and hard.*

HILARY. Do you think they can do it?

DORCAS. Don't know.

HILARY. Laces seemed pretty confident yesterday.

DORCAS. The way he operates.

HILARY. Be interesting to see how Janet Morris runs.

DORCAS. What do you get out of it if the squad wins?

HILARY. I prefer to use the word when.

DORCAS. When?

HILARY. I will have proved my point. Women are worth the investment. It'll make an impression.

DORCAS. Not Ortolan. You?

HILARY. Onwards and upwards. A place on the board. I want to be one of the people who make decisions. At some stage I'll quit the company and go for a multi-national. The real big boys, the one's who really do have power.

DORCAS. Do people really buy stuff because we use it?

HILARY. Yes. You're very well known. There's already a response and once the ad's released —

DORCAS. Can I see it?

HILARY. Pardon?

DORCAS. Can I see it?

HILARY. I could bring you a tape, if you know anyone with a video.

DORCAS. Got one.

HILARY. Of course. You must miss a lot of things when you're out training.

DORCAS. Watch myself. How I do. How I can be better. I want a gold. However. I want a gold. Nothing I wouldn't do to be in that squad.

HILARY. I'm told that any four of you is a terrific team. That the disadvantage before has been that there's always been a weak link.

DORCAS. Five of us makes it more difficult.

RADIO. Well, welcome back to Gateshead. Our next event, a very important one, the women's 4 x 100 meter relay. The weather still dull and overcast and that's been reflected in the times on the stopwatch, they've been a little slow. And these girls really looking for a fast time. This is a most important relay for them. They've been training together regularly now and they've got tough opposition in the Czechoslovakians who are drawn in Lane 6. Great Britain drawn in Lane 3. In fact the full line up is Sweden on the inside, then outside them Holland, Spain and the very strong looking Czechoslovakian squad. And the Great Britain squad, well the order, Sue Kinder, Pauline Peterson, Muriel Farr and young Janet Morris the seventeen-year-old orphan girl who came in as a last minute replacement for Dorcas Ableman —

DORCAS. She's eighteen, and she's not an orphan.

RADIO. — a new find for the season — so it must be pretty nerve-racking for her this afternoon. Well Sue Kinder goes to the blocks, thumbs up to Dad, of course, all waiting for that and thumbs up from Dad in return. A very reliable first leg runner, Sue Kinder. Starter's gun is up. Away they go. Sue Kinder running smoothly, chasing hard on the Dutch girl outside her, makes up, oh, about a yard, and then the Spanish girl, the Czechoslovakian's out in front, but that's a good leg by Sue Kinder, running to Pauline Peterson who takes the baton. It's a good exchange. Pauline Peterson's got the wind behind her — she's flowing nicely down the back straight. Running very well indeed. She's taken a yard out of the Czechoslovakian girl. The British squad moving very well and she comes up to Muriel Farr and that's another good exchange. The British squad looking very, very good indeed. Muriel Farr on that bend going hammer and tongs. She's overtaken the rest. It's only Czechoslovakia and they're down and what can Janet Morris do now? She's got the baton safely. Three good exchanges and she's got a yard and a half in front. Now the British squad have really got it together for the first time. Can she hang on to that yard and a half and I'm sure she's going to make it to the line and indeed she does make it to the line. That's a marvellous run.

The British squad really getting it together there and look at the watch! A remarkable forty-one seconds.

HILARY. Is it a remarkable time?

RADIO. A new British record and pretty close to the world record. Now clearly these girls have benefited enormously by getting together day after day in coaching, their sponsorship has paid off.

HILARY. By, by —

RADIO. There really has been a tremendous improvement. What about the seventeen-year-old orphan girl on the last leg? Janet Morris, standing in for Dorcas Ableman.

HILARY. Do you know the number for Gateshead?

DORCAS *is upside down.*

RADIO. Well, it paid off; it really was a remarkable run; a brave run from her. And if these girls show the same form at Crystal Palace in the final trials, I must say this team looks good for medals in Athens.

HILARY. I should have made sure I sent a representative. There must be an area manager or something who could get flowers if he's not playing golf. (HILARY *turns the radio off.*)

DORCAS *begins to cry.*

HILARY. I'm sorry. I know you wanted to run. (HILARY *goes.*)

DORCAS *cries then sings.*

DORCAS. He is the righteous Saviour,
And he shall speak,
He shall speak Peace, Peace,
He shall speak Peace
Unto the heathen.

DORCAS *begins to swallow some pills.*

ACT TWO

Scene One

Heathrow Airport: departure for Athens.

VIVIEN, HILARY, LACES, NOËL, MURIEL, JANET, SUE, DORCAS, PAULINE, TOM, MIKE, THE GOLDEN GIRL.

Flash bulb then lights. The squad are having their photo taken.

PHOTOGRAPHER (*off*). Smile again.

PAULINE. Can't you take one with Split Second in his new outfit?

SUE. They won't let him back in, you know. There'll be a rabies scare.

Flash.

HILARY. Think that you've already won!

Flash.

PHOTOGRAPHER. O.K!

TOM. You certainly know what you are doing.

HILARY. It's my job.

TOM. Is the company satisfied with its investment?

HILARY. There's an identification process certainly. People remember the ad. It's been popular. Sue Kinder's quite a star.

TOM. She's blossomed.

VIVIEN. They'll go to pieces if I take it away now. You know what they're like. Any change in their routine.

LACES. I'm twitchy. I accept it works, but I wish we could find an excuse.

VIVIEN. Are you unhappy with all that I've been doing?

LACES. It's been wonderful.

VIVIEN. They could actually win, they should actually win. Dorcas at Crystal Palace. I wish I wasn't the sort of person who had to know where their passport was every five minutes. (*She looks in her bag.*)

HILARY. I like to know what's going on.

TOM. Don't you trust them behind your back?

HILARY. They wear our logo.

TOM. Sponsors have been very cagey since the Milk Race. Drugged cyclist dying.

HILARY. There you are. Do you blame us? We have a lot invested.

TOM. How much?

Silence.

HILARY. A sports journalist.

TOM. I'm thinking of branching out. It's the investigative boys get all the kudos. If I could just find something in Golden Girls which was smelly, nasty. Your track record is so clean.

She smiles at him.

HILARY. Good as gold.

TOM. I need a scandal for my career. You wouldn't like dinner in Athens this evening?

HILARY. That's a scandal?

THE GOLDEN GIRL. O.K.

HILARY. Is this the one with me in?

PHOTOGRAPHER (*off*). Two seconds.

HILARY. They're all fit?

VIVIEN. Barring accidents and tummy bugs.

HILARY. You don't have anything, well, you know — flying. I know it's totally irrational that planes just don't drop out of the sky.

PHOTOGRAPHER. O.K.

HILARY is to have her photo taken.

She is flanked by SUE and THE GOLDEN GIRL.

Just bring your hair forward over your shoulder —

NOËL crosses to brush SUE's hair.

TOM. They say you've worked them out a wonderful diet.

VIVIEN. They've been doing a lot of hard work. A relay team's never had a chance to spend so long together.

TOM. That the secret?

Camera flash.

VIVIEN. It's a technical race. Won or lost on the moment when the baton changes hands. They know the other girls' palms as well as their own. From the touch to the grasp. That and the fact that they're all terrific runners in their own right.

Camera flash.

TOM. You sound as if you've had nothing to do with it.

VIVIEN. I'm a backroom boy.

TOM. What happens while you're on this jaunt?

VIVIEN. Annual holiday.

TOM. For which you're getting paid?

VIVIEN. I won't come home out of pocket.

HILARY (*launching into a speech for the assembled*).

Ladies and gentlemen. If you like to see that you've got a glass. I would just like to say how pleased we are that these girls are running for Britain and for Ortolan —

DORCAS. One hundred pounds.

MURIEL. Can you remember what her total is?

JANET. Can't be anywhere near Sue's.

DORCAS. That's because Sue gets all the interviews.

HILARY. Ortolan —

MURIEL. Two hundred pounds.

HILARY. — is proud to have been able to let these girls have a chance to develop into a team, a real team, and —

P.A. British Airways announces the departure of Flight BA 349 to Amsterdam.

HILARY. And we're just as much in the dark as anyone as to whom the final team is likely to be. Dorcas Ableman's fantastic run at Crystal Palace has really thrown the whole issue into the melting pot. So if you would all like to raise your glasses, I would just like to wish the squad good luck, *bon voyage*, and the Midas touch.

Camera flashes.

VIVIEN. She's had her ginger?

NOËL. She's not bad on planes.

LACES. Got your boarding passes?

NOËL. Mine, Sue's.

LACES. Any more for duty free, do it now.

NOËL. Sue, love, smile.

MIKE. Excited?

JANET. Yes. I want to see it all. All tiny cars.

MIKE. The Alps are spectacular.

JANET. Aunty gave me a St Christopher. Stupid, she doesn't believe in saints.

MIKE. Did you take the toothpaste?

DORCAS. Yes.

MIKE. What am I supposed to use?

JANET. You can have mine.

DORCAS. They do have toothpaste in Greece.

MURIEL. I've left George a quiche; after that he's on his own with the freezer.

JANET. He never comes to watch?

MURIEL. Too busy. Hi-fi firms don't run themselves.

MIKE. Hey, that's our plane. Look.

JANET. Seeing I'm the only one who hasn't flown, do you think they'll let me sit by the window?

TOM. I gather you're buying a house so you can be nearer the centre.

SUE. That's right, Tom.

TOM. Must be quite a difference after the prices up North.

SUE. You're telling me.

TOM. Mortgage?

SUE. I'm not earning.

TOM. Then you still regard yourself as an amateur?

SUE. Aren't I? Who wants to go pro? Tax, accountants, all that sort of hassle.

TOM. So it's more profitable being an amateur?

SUE. Oh no. Just like there are no politics.

TOM. You're a bright girl.

SUE. Just because I've got it in my legs doesn't mean I haven't got it up here.

TOM. Who are they going to drop?

SUE. I beg your pardon?

TOM. I thought that after Gateshead that Dorcas was the obvious one. But after her time at Crystal Palace.

DORCAS *separates* MURIEL *from the rest.*

DORCAS. Have you said anything?

MURIEL. No.

DORCAS. It is discrimination.

MURIEL. You can't prove it.

DORCAS. I've seen the ad. It's all Sue Kinder and the Golden Girl. All we are is little black dots. She signs the cheques. She gets what she wants. And what she wants is four Sue Kinder clones. Since she can't have that, two black, two white is the obvious compromise.

LACES. Boarding passes.

MURIEL. Ta.

LACES. I've assumed you wanted Mike to sit beside you to hold your hand.

DORCAS. We want a word about the squad.

LACES. Nothing is decided.

DORCAS. But you know the team you would like?

LACES. Perhaps not here, Dorcas.

DORCAS. Why's Muriel out?

LACES. No one is out.

DORCAS. Me, Sue, Pauline and Janet — with Muriel as reserve. Isn't that the plan?

LACES. Five into four isn't simple mathematics. A thousand things between then and now. Who's to say what might happen in the individuals?

DORCAS. Sue's a lousy starter.

LACES. She's made a lot of progress this season.

DORCAS. Don't you want a team that will win?

LACES. Any combination of you could. You're all well within the qualifying time. Who says this one won't.

DORCAS. It's the slowest.

LACES. I don't accept that.

DORCAS. What if we go and talk to Madame?

LACES. If you get a sponsor you don't upset them.

DORCAS. So that is what's happened.

LACES. I had to pick some sort of team. A rough list, not a final decision.

DORCAS. You can't just —

LACES. Are you offering to be reserve?

DORCAS. No.

LACES. O.K.

DORCAS. It isn't fair.

LACES. No one ever said it was. I'm sorry Muriel but your times are least consistent.

MURIEL. Since when?

LACES. The team stands. (*He goes.*)

DORCAS. Since when?

MURIEL. He's not going to change it.

DORCAS. He will.

MURIEL. Oh leave it. The longer it's set to work out the change-overs the better.

DORCAS. No.

MURIEL. It's going to look like a personal feud.

DORCAS. If you don't care.

MURIEL. I don't know. I don't want a fuss. It's not that I don't care but —

DORCAS. We're being pushed around.

MURIEL. We can't prove it.

DORCAS. It doesn't need a witness box. What's Sue's personal best this season?

MURIEL. You're pretending you don't know.

DORCAS. At Crystal Palace I wasn't even looking for her.

JANET *returns.*

JANET. If Sue put on all those fancy clothes she'd look just like the Golden Girl.

DORCAS. You have to run.

MURIEL. I've got my own event.

DORCAS. Our event. The team. Sue's not part of it. She never has been. She doesn't belong with us.

MURIEL. Let's forget it. O.K? (*She starts to go.*)

DORCAS. You did the best time in the world last year.

MURIEL. Laces thinks I'm not consistent.

DORCAS. Are you?

MURIEL. Look —

DORCAS. What do you want?

    Pause.

MURIEL. I don't know.

DORCAS. You do. (*She holds* MURIEL *threateningly.*)

MURIEL. My last chance. I want to run.

    Camera flash.

DORCAS. O.K.

    DORCAS *lets go of* MURIEL.

MURIEL. How?

DORCAS. Madame first, I suppose.

MURIEL. She'll just say it's Laces.

DORCAS. We find a reporter. Someone who knows what they're talking about and we talk. Tom Billbow, someone like that. Someone with a mouth they don't mind shooting off.

JANET. We should refuse to run.

DORCAS. What?

JANET. Refuse to run.

DORCAS. We'd be suspended.

    NOËL *crosses to* TOM.

NOËL. Will you be using Sue's photo?

    TOM *shrugs.*

TOM. Black girls at each others' throats. Which would you use?

NOËL. You a cheque book journalist?

TOM. Why? You got something you want to sell?

NOËL. Just wondered.

TOM. The problem is people sell you the story you're buying.

NOËL. I used to like your column.

TOM. People don't know who I am any more.

P.A. Flight BA 128 for Athens now boarding at Gate Four.

NOËL. Sue.

SUE. O.K. O.K.

A song from the group as they leave.

LACES. I won't have it.

DORCAS. We weren't fighting.

LACES. Where are your spikes?

JANET. In my case.

LACES. Have you never heard stories of cases going astray and ending up in the middle of nowhere?

MIKE. You'd better pee. There's something about aircraft loos makes it difficult.

LACES. Go on. Before it goes without you.

JANET and MIKE go.

PAULINE. Do I have to guess who I'm sitting next to?

LACES . I know Split Second likes to have a window seat.

PAULINE goes.

HILARY comes back.

HILARY. There are already questions. I think it would be an idea for you two to sit together. Nip any rumours in the bud.

MURIEL. It wasn't a fight. (MURIEL *goes.*)

LACES. Even after Crystal Palace you aren't so untouchable that you can't be dropped.

DORCAS. There'd be questions.

HILARY. We'd have answers.

DORCAS. You need me.

HILARY. There's a point where we'd be losing more than we're gaining.

DORCAS. You pick and choose us.

HILARY. I sign cheques. I know nothing about athletics.

DORCAS. Exactly.

LACES. Shall we just see how it goes in Athens?

DORCAS goes.

HILARY. I'm not the one who should have to deal with this.

LACES. I'll sort it out.

HILARY. I hope so.

LACES. There's a lot of tension, they've put in a lot of effort. I don't think you appreciate —

HILARY. I don't like flying. I'd appreciate my hand being held.

She goes.

LACES. What happens to you?

THE GOLDEN GIRL. No one's said. I suppose I just get changed and go. (*She gathers up her things.*)

LACES. I'll give you a hand.

The stage is empty for a few seconds. MIKE and JANET enter.

MIKE. Dorcas is just hyped up, that's all.

JANET. Do you think I should offer to be reserve?

MIKE. No. You're very good.

JANET. You're fabulous.

MIKE. Not the best.

JANET. I believe in you.

MIKE. I'll get a paunch like Laces' in the end.

JANET. You won't. (*They kiss.*)

LACES *sees.*

LACES. You're a fool.

Pause.

What are you?

MIKE. A fool.

LACES. As if she hasn't got enough.

MIKE. I'm not a machine.

LACES. I don't mean to sound like a school teacher, but the next two weeks are going to need every ounce of your concentration. Kudos, is it? Mike Bassett?

MIKE. She didn't chase.

LACES. Do you think it's clever.

JANET. My life.

LACES. Yes. It could be called unfortunate. Get on that plane.

(*She goes.*)

Mike, there are certain times in your career when you just don't blow it —

MIKE. She believes in me.

LACES. — whatever the temptation. You have to do that for yourself. Have you never learned?

MIKE. I injure badly.

LACES. A hypochondriac looking for excuses. Mike, you won't win in Athens, do you know that?

MIKE. I could win.

LACES. You have to give running one hundred per cent. If you prefer the other, that's your choice; but you are on the way down, Mike.

MIKE. She doesn't think I'm on the way down.

LACES. It's called flattery. It makes you feel important. I'm not denying it feels good, but she's eighteen.

MIKE. She has her own mind.

LACES. And she has to focus it. And what about Dorcas?

MIKE. They can't crack it anyway.

LACES. A good day, the right conditions — forty dead is not impossible. It is just difficult to contemplate, the women as quick as the men.

MIKE. The men's team is lousy.

LACES. The women have always been slower.

MIKE. Laces Mackenzie blows sport wide open!

LACES. Yes. Shush! That relay team. Any combination, magic.

MIKE. You don't believe in magic.

LACES. I believe in them.

P.A. This is the final call for Flight BA 128 for Athens, now boarding at Gate Four.

They go.

THE GOLDEN GIRL *crosses, without the gear she looks drab, dreary and ordinary.*

Scene Two

Greece at night. A terrace above Athens.

JANET. So much to see and they shut you in.

MURIEL. Safety. The Olympics in Munich. And a sporting ideal. Comrades in competition.

JANET. I hate being in there behind that wire. The world cut in little shapes like a jigsaw. You run to be free. Not to share a room and smell other people's pumps at night.

MURIEL. Is there a problem sharing with Dorcas?

JANET. She's got these funny habits. There's a special order she has to do everything in.

MURIEL. It'll happen to you. One big win and you'll start looking for what it was made it happen.

JANET. Never.

MURIEL. She's O.K. Don't try and chat that's all.

JANET. Some of the men are in hotels.

MURIEL. It's been said time and time again.

Some music from the town can be heard.

JANET. I'd like to have a good time. Just let go —

MURIEL. Ruin it for the rest? Just nerves. You'll be O.K. You're a natural. You don't have to think of where you're putting your feet. Just do everything, everything as it always has been.

JANET. I'd like to go in the dark. Just run. See where I was when the morning came.

MURIEL. The countryside?

JANET. Yes. Here's like anywhere else. All those lights on. Could be Liverpool.

MURIEL. It's a good track.

JANET. I thought it would be more special. As a place I mean.

MURIEL. Hot.

JANET. I mean different. Really different. Not Coca Cola. Greece is supposed to be historic. That's what they'll say about us isn't it. If we crack the British men's record. We made history.

MURIEL. Perhaps.

JANET. I'm going to make history, Greece. Do you hear that? (*She raises her arms and shouts.*) Me. Here. History! (*The words echo.*) You see, it knows. (*She lowers her arms.*) I hate the shirts. So sticky.

MURIEL. Team shirts.

JANET. Why do you do it?

MURIEL *shrugs.*

MURIEL. Way of life.

JANET. Really though?

Pause.

MURIEL. I want that tape to come home to. The moment when it breaks. That moment. (MURIEL *slowly lifts her arms. She wraps them round herself.*

She sighs.)

JANET. What?

MURIEL. Lonely, that's all. Lonely inside.

JANET. What?

MURIEL. Nothing.

Enter VIVIEN *and* HILARY.

HILARY. Look, I'm really starting to catch the sun.

Moment.

VIVIEN. What was supper like?

MURIEL. O.K.

VIVIEN. You eat?

JANET. Yes.

VIVIEN. Good. And it's going to be an early night?

MURIEL. You can't sleep for the noise.

VIVIEN. Do you want something for it?

MURIEL. No.

VIVIEN. I could give you something very mild. Hardly an asprin.

MURIEL. I said no!

HILARY. Surely a good night's sleep —

MURIEL. That racket. If you want a return on your investment you could put us in a hotel where the rooms are sound-proofed.

HILARY. Are you having problems?

JANET. It's all fine. Great! Smashing!

HILARY. Good. And you're feeling confident about the heats?

JANET. Yes.

VIVIEN. Don't go all out.

JANET. You sound like Laces.

VIVIEN. I'm meant to.

MURIEL. She's a natural.

VIVIEN. There's no fun in being too certain.

HILARY. I'm relying on you not to let me down. I want to go to the board next week and put four gold medals on the table and say 'Look, I was right'.

JANET. Our medals?

HILARY. You'll get them back.

JANET. I'm wearing mine. Twenty-four hours a day I'm wearing it.

MURIEL. They're hell when you're trying to sleep.

Pause.

The gold comes off. Did you know that? They're plated. They tarnish.

VIVIEN. Let's get through the heats shall we before we start discussing how long the medals are going to last. Beautiful, isn't it?

JANET. If you look down there you can see the board with the events.

JANET *and* VIVIEN *go.*

HILARY. You must be pleased with your time this afternoon?

MURIEL. The fastest qualifier. A lot of people would see that as an ill omen.

HILARY. Really?

MURIEL. Giving your all before the big race. You are supposed to hold back. Do just as much as necessary.

HILARY. You miss-timed it?

MURIEL. I wanted to be sure I made the final.

HILARY. What do you reckon your chances are there?

MURIEL. Pauline ran just the right race this afternoon, she'll have an advantage over me.

HILARY. Are athletes always pessimists?

MURIEL. So many things to go wrong.

Enter DORCAS.

DORCAS. I bet Barbados is like this. Warm at night. My Ma said there were crickets there, used to cheep all night. Dad says she's just imagining it. He's forgotten which side of the road the cars go on.

HILARY. Cicadas.

DORCAS. Pardon?

HILARY. Cicadas, in the trees, not crickets. In Barbados.

DORCAS. You went there?

HILARY. On holiday once.

DORCAS. What was it like?

HILARY. There was a typhoon. Sand got everywhere. I itched for days.

DORCAS. What side did the cars go on?

HILARY tries to remember.

HILARY. I'll tell you when it comes back to me.

DORCAS. My Ma got pregnant with me in Christchurch. Just my luck to get born in Dagenham.

Enter MIKE.

Pause.

HILARY. Bad luck.

MIKE. Thanks.

MURIEL. Still your relay.

VIVIEN. Hilary, come and look at this.

HILARY goes.

Pause.

MURIEL. You can see the board above the stadium. (*She goes.*)

Pause.

DORCAS. I can't take it Mike. Not tonight.

MIKE. It's the end.

DORCAS. It's always like that when you lose. Get it together, another race.

MIKE Lose again. Knowing that they're waiting for it.

DORCAS. I don't want to hear. Not tonight.

MIKE. I want to talk to you. Right? (*Pause.*) I had to win.

DORCAS. You didn't.

MIKE. How many million people saw me with tears running down my cheeks.

DORCAS. Television doesn't show the losers. You start too slowly to get it back trying to accelerate on the curve.

MIKE. Any school coach would tell me that.

DORCAS. Then you know.

MIKE. I want to win and I can't.

DORCAS. English born and bred, you're supposed to be a good loser.

MIKE. Talk to me.

DORCAS. I can't.

Pause.

But I need you there watching me.

MIKE. I lost.

DORCAS. I need you there.

Enter JANET.

JANET. Our toothbrushes are the same. Mine's in the glass. (*She hands* MIKE *a tube of toothpaste.*) She and I can share the toothpaste. Don't let it get to you.

MIKE. Not here.

DORCAS. Shooting stars! (*They look*).

You're supposed to wish. (*They look. Nothing.*)

JANET. Wish me luck.

MIKE. You don't need it.

JANET. Will you watch?

MIKE. I promised Dorcas.

Pause.

JANET. When we get back.

MIKE. I'm not sure.

JANET. You promised.

MIKE. I don't know. Dorcas'll guess.

JANET. I don't care.

MIKE. I don't want her hurt.

JANET. Enough. You said you'd had enough.

DORCAS. There! (DORCAS *points*.)

MIKE. No.

Enter SUE *and* NOËL *with ice creams.*

NOËL. Have you tried the ices?

MIKE. No time.

NOËL. Bad luck. Up to the girls to fly the flag.

MIKE. Yes.

NOËL. I thought I saw a Bee Eater this afternoon. But the bird
books here are all in Greek. The sort of place for Night Jars.

MIKE. I thought I heard something up there in the trees.

MIKE and NOËL *go.*

SUE. Awful luck with the draw.

DORCAS. The heats are supposed to be even.

SUE. They can't change them now, it would be admitting the
draw was wrong. I don't suppose you have a problem with the
heat.

JANET. I'm sweating something awful.

SUE. Has Vivien given you some salt?

JANET. No.

SUE. You ought to have some.

JANET. I'll ask her. (JANET *goes*.)

SUE. D'you want a taste?

Pause.

DORCAS. Thanks. (DORCAS *takes a lick of* SUE's *ice cream*.)

Enter TOM.

TOM. How touching.

SUE. You're a sweet man and I know you're very keen but we've a big day tomorrow —

TOM. O.K., I understand.

He creeps off.

DORCAS. Room O.K?

SUE. Never share with a swimmer! It's wet bathing costumes and those horrid little rubber hats everywhere. What's the kid like?

DORCAS. At least she's tidy. You know what it's like with Pauline, stuff everywhere.

SUE. One of these days someone'll put themselves out falling over her junk.

Nervous?

DORCAS. Yes. You?

SUE. Yes. What do you think of the kid's chances?

DORCAS. She's the unknown.

SUE. She's got quite a crush on Mike.

DORCAS. We call her the Lamb.

NOËL (*calling*). Sue!

SUE. I can't see the bloody things hiding in the trees in the daytime let alone the dark.

DORCAS. As far as I'm concerned they're all sparrows or blackbirds.

SUE. Once you get obsessed there are different sorts of sparrows.

Enter JANET.

JANET. She says she'll get me some.

SUE. Good.

JANET. If we were film stars we'd have our names up there in lights. Not just our events.

NOËL (*calling*). Sue!

SUE *shrugs to* DORCAS.

SUE. It's like playing I-spy. (*She goes.*)

JANET. Poor Mike eh?

DORCAS. Don't give him sympathy. Make him run for it.

JANET. But crying.

DORCAS. Don't you think you might have something to do with it?

JANET. You what?

DORCAS. It doesn't bother me. Just keep him off my back until after this. And a bit of discretion. I couldn't handle people wanting stories.

Enter MURIEL.

MURIEL. You haven't seen Tom Billbow?

DORCAS. He's sniffing around here somewhere.

Enter MIKE.

MIKE. I thought I'd have an ice. At least I'm not off my food.

JANET. I'm so excited it just disappears. I'm really hungry all the time.

MIKE. Have an ice.

JANET. I think I might. Do they do chocolate?

MIKE. Don't know.

MURIEL. Why don't you go with him and choose your own?

MIKE. Do you want one Dorcas?

She shakes her head.

JANET. Come on. (JANET *and* MIKE *go*.)

MURIEL. Can you remember when it used to be fun like that?

DORCAS. Still is. Isn't it?

MURIEL. The running of the races.

DORCAS. If it isn't you should quit.

MURIEL. I know.

DORCAS. We could get a relay gold.

MURIEL. It's not up to us.

DORCAS. Yes, it is.

   Enter HILARY *and* VIVIEN.

HILARY. I'll have to go in. I don't know what they ate before I got here. The cars are the same as at home. I'm almost certain. It's British after all.

VIVIEN. Have you seen Janet?

DORCAS. Buying some ice cream.

VIVIEN. I could never have eaten ice cream the night before my heat.

MURIEL. She has no nerves.

HILARY. I think I'm doing the worrying for her.

   Enter NOËL *and* SUE.

NOËL. You're hearing things. Nightingales don't sing at this time of year.

VIVIEN. Early nights?

NOËL. She's on her way.

MURIEL. Pauline went to bed hours ago.

VIVIEN. There'll be plenty of time to savour the atmosphere once the heats are over.

SUE. We'll have the finals.

HILARY. I'm glad someone is an optimist.

MURIEL. Have you seen a phone box anywhere?

HILARY. Is there one in the taverna?

MURIEL (*looking at her watch*). He mightn't be home yet. Still worth a try. (*She goes.*)

HILARY. I'm going to be eaten alive. Coming?

VIVIEN. I'd like to give Janet her salt before she goes to bed.

DORCAS. Give it to me. I'll give it to her.

VIVIEN. Of course, you're sharing.

DORCAS. Night.

SUE. Night.

VIVIEN *and* DORCAS *go.*

HILARY. We don't want bags under those eyes. Not if she wants to be considered as the new Golden Girl. (HILARY *goes.*)

SUE *stands.*

SUE. Why can't she leave me alone?

NOËL. Come on. Bed.

Pause.

SUE. Listen!

Pause.

NOËL. You heard what Miss Davenport said?

SUE. I want to stay.

NOËL. You've a race tomorrow.

SUE. I know. Outside at night and it's warm.

NOËL. I'm not staying up here all night.

SUE. Go.

NOËL. I'm going to get cross.

SUE. Get cross.

NOËL. I'll tell Laces.

SUE. What's he going to do? Come and fetch me?

NOËL. You don't like the dark.

SUE. This isn't dark. Listen!

Pause.

NOËL. I'm going.

SUE. Go. I can do it for myself now, Dad.

She stands her ground. He is forced to go.

A moment. Possibly we hear the bird. Enter MURIEL.

I'd like to stay for the dawn. If I hadn't got a heat. It's so easy running in the sun. The outside as warm as in. Heaven.

MURIEL. Whenever I'm away I want to go home. To go somewhere to be still. To be able to shut the door.

SUE goes.

MURIEL stands for a moment. Enter TOM.

TOM. Doesn't it worry you? A girl up here on your own? You know what they say about Greek men?

MURIEL. I can look after myself.

TOM belches.

TOM. Pardon. Greek wine is filthy but I can claim it is scotch. I was impressed this afternoon.

MURIEL. Thank you.

TOM. Can you do it?

MURIEL. Who can ever say?

TOM. Are you beginning to think of quitting?

MURIEL. Sometimes. (*Pause.*) I wanted a word.

TOM. With me?

MURIEL . Yes, I think so. (*Pause.*) It's a sort of question really. I hope you don't mind.

TOM. I'm flattered to be asked.

MURIEL. It's about Heidi Lynikova.

TOM. Yes.

MURIEL. There are stories in the camp —

TOM. Isn't gossip always rife amongst you?

MURIEL. Please.

TOM. I beg your pardon.

MURIEL. You know she was pregnant when she smashed the record in Oslo?

TOM. Fanny Blankers-Cohen in 1948 all over again.

MURIEL. Did you ever hear about the baby? (TOM *thinks*.) It had everything wrong with it. They say it was a freak.

TOM. Really?

MURIEL. The American girls say it had something to do with some stuff she was taking. I wondered if you knew.

TOM. Why?

Pause.

MURIEL *produces a capsule.*

TOM. Oh!

MURIEL. It's legitimate. At least in the sense that nothing shows up.

TOM. A wonder drug?

MURIEL. We haven't had a bad season.

TOM. I thought it was the presence of Janet Morris amongst you. Youth snapping at your heels. Do you know what it is?

MURIEL. It's called hydro-something.

TOM. It's not cricket.

MURIEL. No. I don't want to stay in this game forever. Even if you want to your body starts to go and lets you down. I want to win here and then children. (*About the drug.*) We're running as fast as some of the men. (TOM *takes it.*) It's not black market stuff. They come from the doctor.

TOM. Paid for by Ortolan?

MURIEL. I suppose so, in a manner of speaking. I thought you might have some way of finding out.

TOM. Hairy chests, anything like that?

MURIEL. It's not a steroid. It's made from rats.

TOM. It could be very messy.

MURIEL. Yes.

TOM. Drug analysis is expensive. The paper's money. They'll expect to be able to make a story.

MURIEL. Yes.

TOM. You'll be pilloried in every paper, every sports club —

MURIEL. Find out what it does. Please. Isn't it what they call a scoop?

TOM. Yes.

Scene Three

Athens.

The team are working on the baton changes. They work in pairs: SUE to PAULINE; MURIEL to JANET; DORCAS on the side lines. LACES watches.

They start with the shout and the change. JANET starts too soon.

LACES. Do that on the day and you'll be out of the box without thinking about it.

JANET. Sorry.

LACES. You've to be absolutely certain of the moment to go. (*The other change-over has gone well.*) Well done.

SUE. Thanks.

LACES. Try moving your mark back — just about a meter.

   JANET *does.*

MURIEL. Louder shout?

LACES. Give it as much as you can.

   They do it again and it is better but JANET looks back after she has started her run.

LACES. Don't look back.

PAULINE. It's so hot. Dripping off me.

SUE. Think what it will be like with the tension.

PAULINE. Don't.

LACES. If it's sweaty get a dry one on. You can get chills even at this temperature.

SUE. What was that like?

PAULINE. The baton was just too far forward. I'd have had problems on my hand over. (*She demonstrates.*) If you could just take your hand fractionally back along it.

SUE. The problem with that is starting. (SUE *tries to work out her start with the baton in the new position in her hand.*)

PAULINE. Perhaps it's just me. We always did the downward pass at school.

SUE. You see the problem is there. Hang on. (*She goes through several repeats.*)

LACES. O.K. Dorcas, you come in as outgoing runner.

DORCAS. Give me a few.

MURIEL. Hand. (MURIEL *does a few slow motion movements of the baton into* DORCAS's *hand.*)

MURIEL. Hand. My hand's so sticky. Hand.

DORCAS. O.K.

LACES. Ready?

DORCAS. Is this supposed to represent the edge of the box?

LACES. Yes.

DORCAS. Can you put something there so I can see it when I come up to it?

LACES *puts a bit of clothing, or something, there.*

LACES. O.K?

DORCAS. Great. Thanks. (*To* MURIEL.) Right?

MURIEL. Right?

DORCAS *counts back — and makes her mark.*

HILARY *enters.*

LACES (*to* JANET). Watch this.

DORCAS. You giving the go?

LACES *signals to* MURIEL. *The whole thing takes place perfectly.*

HILARY. Was that good?

LACES. About as good as it ever can be.

HILARY. Congratulations.

LACES. Look, whatever it is I don't want to hear here and now. We've only got another 30 minutes.

HILARY. Can I watch?

LACES. Of course.

SUE *and* PAULINE *set up to go again.*

SUE. Hand!

PAULINE *misses the baton.*

PAULINE. Shit!

LACES. What happened?

PAULINE. Slipped.

SUE. Another go?

PAULINE. Do you mind?

SUE. It's O.K.

They go again.

SUE. Hand!

Again PAULINE *drops the baton.*

LACES. Have you gone to pieces?

PAULINE. No.

LACES. Then what?

SUE. I thought you had it.

PAULINE. I did.

SUE. Try spraying your palms with deodorant.

PAULINE. Have you got some?

SUE, *of course, has.*

DORCAS. Can we call it a day?

LACES. You happy with that?

DORCAS. Fine. (*To* MURIEL.) Have you got any problems?

MURIEL. No.

LACES. I'd just like to have a look at Janet to Pauline.

JANET. Fine.

DORCAS *and* MURIEL *stay to watch this.*

LACES. Don't stand there like muffins. Set it out for yourselves. I won't be down there in the heats tomorrow.

JANET *and* PAULINE *go about setting their marks.*

HILARY. Have you finally decided?

LACES. Not yet. Why?

HILARY. It's just that it would be nice if there was the same balance in the team as there is in the advertisement — two black and two white girls.

LACES. I think you'll find you need it further back than that.

PAULINE. You aren't going to be down there on the track tomorrow.

They get ready.

LACES. Just the change. That's all. Ready?

They go.

JANET. Hand!

PAULINE *drops the baton.* LACES *is beside himself.*

LACES. What the hell is the matter with you? (PAULINE *just stands and shakes her head.*) Go. (*The others do.*) And you. (HILARY *goes.*) If it's something I can do. Tell me.

PAULINE. She just doesn't give me enough.

LACES. Janet or Sue?

PAULINE. I've blown it, haven't I?

LACES. Of course not.

PAULINE. Three drops one after the other.

LACES. I don't make snap judgements. I find the reason then decide.

PAULINE. I'd rather just know.

LACES. As soon as I make the decision to drop you, I'll let you know, O.K? So don't stand there and come that with me. I know the screws are on and it's all getting tighter and tighter — are you sleeping?

PAULINE. Yes.

LACES. Even without taking anything?

PAULINE. All that stuff Vivien's done about talking to myself.

Pause.

LACES. Is it that you know and you're not going to say?

Pause.

Something to do with the squad? (*She shakes her head.*) Are they pressurising you? Dorcas's plan for three black girls together?

PAULINE. They're all better than me.

LACES. Muriel ran a silly race yesterday. She's probably used all she's got. You ran it exactly right. You've got something left over.

PAULINE. Just let me be the reserve, O.K.

LACES. If I think you're good enough to run, you'll run.

PAULINE. I don't want to be picked just because you fancy me. I know I'm not good enough.

LACES. I run you in the relay squad because I think you're good. Because you have technique at your finger-tips.

PAULINE. Butter fingers!

MURIEL *comes back. She protects* PAULINE.

LACES. It's a crisis of confidence. (*Pause.*) I didn't mean to shout at you. I'm sorry.

PAULINE. Shout at me. Tell me I'm no good. Tell me the truth. (PAULINE *cries.*)

LACES. You are a very, very good runner. You have text-book technique. I do like you a lot. But if you think another coach would help perhaps that's what had better happen. (*He goes.*)

MURIEL *stands with* PAULINE.

PAULINE. I'm hopeless.

MURIEL. That's what you say about learning to drive.

PAULINE. He fancies me and Madame wants as many white runners as possible. That's the only reason I'm in. I know I'm no good.

MURIEL. This is silly. I'm not going to listen to it.

PAULINE *gradually calms down.*

Enter TOM.

TOM. Something up?

PAULINE. Sky! Don't want Split Second getting sun stroke. (*She takes Split Second and goes.*)

TOM. I take it we have a team?

MURIEL. Don't jump to conclusions.

TOM. I'd call tears conclusive.

MURIEL. Well?

TOM. Not Hydromel.

MURIEL. What?

TOM. Completely rodent free. (*He hands her a piece of paper.*)

TOM. The Greek analysis.

MURIEL. This is impossible.

TOM. That's what they say it is.

MURIEL. We're turning in results as if we'd got a following wind and this says we're taking the ingredients of a cake mix. It doesn't make sense.

TOM. No. London have their doubts about the Greek labs. They'd like to get some back and get them analysed properly. I have to have some more.

MURIEL. She'd know.

TOM. Five, one off each of you.

Pause.

MURIEL. I'll try.

TOM. You'll get them to me?

MURIEL. Yes.

TOM. You can reach me at my hotel. The Acropolis. It's all reinforced concrete. I could take you out to eat if you like.

MURIEL. No thanks. The butterflies get the better of the menu.

Exit TOM.

At school I was always the fastest runner. From I don't remember when. George would understand boxing. He'd like a boy to be a boxer. I like the tape to come home to. The moment when you dip and no one has to tell you that you've won. When all the waiting and all the effort's been worthwhile. The winning. The peace of it all being over. Then the pain comes back. The tightening of the thighs and pins and needles in the heels. Once I looked at my feet and could see blood coming through my shoes. And you smile and smile because it doesn't matter. Nothing matters. One would do it again and again and not count the cost. Until there was something you wanted more.

Scene Four

Athens. The athletes' camp.

Everyone is bored. It is the morning before the big race; SUE is sun bathing and MURIEL is writing post cards. MIKE is reading about community access to educational sports facilities. NOËL has binoculars and a bird book. JANET is testing PAULINE on her highway code. DORCAS plays solitaire, obsessively, and LACES paces.

SUE. What time is it?

NOËL. Quarter to.

JANET. Blue square, then in the middle of it is like a 'T' and the top of the 'T' is red.

MIKE. It's easy.

PAULINE. I'm thinking.

MURIEL. My road?

PAULINE. Dead end?

JANET. Yes. Red triangle —

Enter VIVIEN.

VIVIEN. You'll get dehydrated.

SUE *sips her drink.*

JANET. With white in the middle and sort of rock?

PAULINE. Danger falling rocks.

LACES. Can you have a look at Janet's hamstring? It's a bit tender.

VIVIEN. Of course. (VIVIEN *goes to* JANET.)

LACES (*to* SUE). I just want to talk you through your start.

SUE. Trust my back foot, trust my grip, trust myself.

LACES. Good girl. Are you happy with the change-over to Muriel.

SUE. I have to be.

LACES. You know what you're going to do if she wrong foots?

SUE. She won't.

LACES. But if she does?

SUE. You're giving me something to worry about that I don't need to.

VIVIEN. Is that better?

JANET. A bit.

VIVIEN. There's not much else I can do, I'm afraid. All I can do is promise you some pain killers when it's all over.

LACES *goes up to* DORCAS.

DORCAS. I get the baton and then I run like the wind. O.K?

LACES. Great. (*He watches her play.*) What will you do if it ever comes out?

DORCAS. It won't.

SUE. What time is it?

NOËL. Ten to.

SUE *turns over.*

SUE. Do me a favour.

PAULINE *starts to rub sun tan lotion on* SUE.

VIVIEN. Any more aches and pains?

NOËL. You'll turn them into hyperchondriacs.

VIVIEN. If I can give them one thing less to worry about — I give them a split second's more concentration.

MIKE *to* DORCAS.

DORCAS. I have to have your chain.

MIKE. I lost.

DORCAS. I still have to have it.

He gives it to her.

Thanks . You will come down to the track?

MIKE. Why?

DORCAS. I want you to see me do it.

MIKE. O.K.

> NOËL *to* SUE.

NOËL. Sue, shall we talk about the start?

SUE. I know what I'm doing.

NOËL. You've got to remember —

SUE. You aren't my coach anymore. (*Pause.*) I'm sorry but I have to have the very best.

NOËL. Him?

SUE. He's taught me things that —

NOËL. I've sold the house. Everything. I'm not asking for thanks but —

SUE. What do you want?

NOËL. I wanted you to have your chance.

SUE. I'm taking it.

> NOËL *moves away.*

MIKE. She's uptight.

NOËL. I don't like being in the south. I don't belong. I wanted her to have her chance.

MIKE. Once we're all back home.

NOËL. My little girl.

LACES (*to* PAULINE). You O.K?

PAULINE. Don't be nice to me.

LACES. Then I don't know what to say.

PAULINE. It's easy. Don't say anything.

LACES. You couldn't have been selected.

PAULINE. I know.

MIKE. Why did they call you Laces?

MURIEL. Yes, tell us.

LACES. It's silly.

JANET. I thought it was your real name.

LACES. School. One day I forgot my laces. Couldn't keep my
shoes on. Couldn't run. The team lost. Put us out of the
running for the shield. Every time the gym teacher saw me
after that he used to shout 'Remember your laces.' I've been
Laces ever since.

VIVIEN. What's your real name?

LACES (*embarrassed*). Lawrence.

DORCAS. Lawrence!

PAULINE. It's no worse than Dorcas.

DORCAS. Dorcas means gazelle.

LACES *looks at his watch.*

LACES. O.K.

The girls start to get up to go.

VIVIEN. Good luck.

DORCAS. We're going to do it. Aren't we? We're going to do it.

The four runners gather in a huddle.

DORCAS. Forty seconds dead!

MURIEL. Forty seconds dead!

JANET. Forty seconds dead!

SUE. Forty seconds dead!

LACES. Let's go!

MURIEL. Come down and watch.

PAULINE. Perhaps.

MURIEL *goes.*

MIKE. I'll be there.

DORCAS. Yes. (*She goes.*)

MIKE (*to* JANET). Don't panic. Wait 'til she hits her mark and
then go like the wind.

JANET. Right. (JANET *goes.*)

VIVIEN. Your big day?

LACES. Could be.

VIVIEN. Will be.

LACES. Thanks.

   VIVIEN *goes.*

SUE. You have to give me the thumbs up.

NOËL. Everything Sue.

SUE. You're still my Dad whether you train me or not. (SUE
   goes.)

   LACES *goes.*

VIVIEN. Well we could all have some lunch? Mr Kinder?

NOËL. Might as well. Kill the time. (*They go.*)

   PAULINE *goes back to her highway code.*

MIKE. Going to pass this time?

PAULINE. Better do.

MIKE. What are you going to do now?

PAULINE. Have another shower. Go down to the track. Wave the
   flag.

MIKE. Back home?

PAULINE. Start training again. Really concentrate. Might change
   coaches. I've never thought of the future, not before I'm
   twenty-five.

MIKE. I'll end up shouting at kids like that guy did at Laces.

PAULINE. You're a good runner. You could still get it back.

MIKE. I don't think I want to. I'll see you down there?

PAULINE. Yes.

   MIKE goes.

   I used to be happy being the best in the street. Then the
   best in the school, best in Kilburn, London, England, Britain,
   Europe, the world. You do one of them you think you'll
   be satisfied. You're still hungry. Do another and it makes
   you hungrier. Every win you think there'll be a feeling

of content. And there isn't. You get up and start all over again. Thinking one day you'll be full.

Enter TOM.

TOM. You can smell the tension.

PAULINE. A lot of people's big day.

TOM. Have you seen Muriel Farr?

PAULINE. Gone down to the track.

TOM. Hell!

PAULINE. Something the matter?

TOM. A few questions about the squad.

PAULINE. There's still me.

   Pause.

TOM. What do you know about Hydromel?

PAULINE. Sounds Greek to me.

TOM. It's a drug.

PAULINE. I don't know anything about no drugs.

TOM. Are you sure?

PAULINE. Yes.

TOM. But you've heard of it?

PAULINE. Yes.

TOM. You know what it does?

PAULINE. Supposed to make you run faster.

TOM. Yes. And the side effects?

PAULINE. Why should I know?

   TOM *gets out a capsule.*

TOM. You recognise it? (*Pause.*) Vivien Blackwood. She's as hungry that the team do well as you are.

PAULINE. It's because we've got it cracked on the baton changes.

TOM. Why aren't you in the team?

PAULINE. I dropped the baton.

TOM. They tell me Hydromel speeds up the physical processes but not altogether consistently. Co-ordination is affected.

PAULINE. You haven't got any proof.

TOM. A lot of evidence.

PAULINE. Proof!

TOM *indicates the drug.*

PAULINE. You could come in here with anything and pretend we swallow it but unless you can get one of us to piss into a jar for you — (*She picks up* SUE's *glass.*) Do it in here for you if you like.

TOM. O.K. It's not you. But if it's not you, it's one of them down there and where does that leave me?

Enter HILARY.

HILARY. I wanted to be here to say good luck.

PAULINE. They had to go.

HILARY. Did they seem bright?

TOM. Feet of clay.

HILARY. I'm sorry?

PAULINE. I have to have lunch. (*She goes.*)

TOM. You know they're taking something?

HILARY. Who?

TOM. Your team.

HILARY. Of course not.

TOM. Didn't Vivien Blackwood promise you winners? (*Pause.*) Everyone cheats in this game, everyone knows. It's not Ancient Greece any more.

HILARY. Don't you know that girls can win. That men can be surprised? I'm going to go into that boardroom and lay four gold medals on the table.

TOM. They're plate. The gold comes off.

Scene Five

The race.

The runners come down the stage passing the baton sideways between them.

Announcement of the race and the start in Greek etc.

They take their tracksuits off. For the first time we see them all in The Golden Girls running stripe.

The race: as they run each girl has one chant in the rhythm of her race.

SUE. Go! Go! (*She repeats until the baton is passed to* MURIEL.)

MURIEL. For me! For me! (*She repeats until the baton is passed to* JANET.)

JANET. Want to win! Want to win! (*She repeats until the baton is passed to* DORCAS.)

DORCAS. Go for it! Go for it! (*She repeats until she goes through the tape and the clock stops.*)

Jubilation; the sound of the stadium; flash bulbs and a moment while they look at their time.

Enter PAULINE.

PAULINE. You were fucking wonderful.

The official time goes up on the scoreboard: 39.99 seconds.

DORCAS. Yes!

JANET. History!

MURIEL *starts to cry.*

MURIEL. I'm just so happy.

SUE. This year's men's record!

Enter MIKE *and* NOËL.

DORCAS. We did it!

MIKE. You were like the wind. Ten second legs!

SUE. You see that Dad? You see that time?

NOËL *take a photo of her.*

MURIEL. If only George was here.

MIKE. I didn't know you could run like that. I never dreamed.

JANET. I've got a gold medal. Me.

   Enter LACES.

SUE (*bugging* LACES). We did it!

LACES. Well done.

NOËL. Is that all you can say?

   LACES *gives* DORCAS *the dope testing card.*

LACES. Short straw I'm afraid. Ableman, Farr, Kinder, Morris —

JANET (*to* DORCAS). I told you you'd get tested in the end!

   Enter HILARY. *She carries a bust crowned with laurel leaves.*

HILARY. I was so excited. Athena, the Goddess of Victory. We wanted to mark the occasion.

SUE. I must have done ten seconds.

LACES. Now!

   LACES *and* MIKE *chair* DORCAS. *As they carry her off, she seizes the bust from* HILARY.

HILARY. The traditional victor's crown. Everybody'll be wanting pictures, stories — Dorcas! (HILARY *goes.*)

SUE. Take that for me, Dad. Take that!

   NOËL *tries to find an angle to get the shot.*

NOËL. You did it for me. The time of my life. (*He goes in order to get the picture.*)

JANET. Fancy having to piss into a jar at a time like this!

PAULINE. Yes, but it's one in the eye for Tom Billbow.

MURIEL. What?

PAULINE. He just never gives up. He says he can prove we're taking Hydromel.

JANET. Nothing showed yesterday.

SUE. Where's he got this from?

PAULINE. If nothing shows up there is no proof.

SUE. Of course there's no proof. We've been taking it and being tested for months.

Enter VIVIEN.

VIVIEN. Did I tell you all? (*She hugs them.*) You must be thrilled.

JANET. I'm getting a gold medal!

Re-enter HILARY *with the wreath back on the bust.*

HILARY (*to* VIVIEN). Congratulations.

VIVIEN. Couldn't have done it without Ortolan.

HILARY (*gathering them to her*). Our Golden Girls.

TANNOY. The medals ceremony of the women's 4 x 100 metres relay has been suspended pending an official enquiry.

Pause.

HILARY. What?

VIVIEN. Some technical hitch. That equipment is very sensitive.

SUE. That stuff you gave us?

VIVIEN. Pardon?

PAULINE. Dorcas has got caught. Hasn't she?

VIVIEN. No.

SUE. I've got to go and be tested.

VIVIEN. Nothing illegal.

MURIEL. Hydromel's not legal. If it was, you wouldn't have told us to keep quiet.

HILARY. You were giving them drugs?

VIVIEN. Nothing that could possibly disqualify them.

SUE. She's been caught.

JANET. I don't know what I'll do if I'm disqualified.

HILARY. Who gave you permission?

VIVIEN. Look at their results.

HILARY. I thought we had made it quite clear. Play by the rules.

VIVIEN. I did.

MURIEL. You doped us.

VIVIEN. No. Never.

SUE. All those pills?

VIVIEN. There was nothing in them.

MURIEL. You told us it was Hydromel.

Pause.

VIVIEN. What I gave you was something called Similexon. A placebo. Flour and sugar in a gelatine shell.

JANET. What's going to happen to me in there?

PAULINE. Just one of us Tom Billbow said.

VIVIEN. Did he say what?

PAULINE. Hydromel! What you told us it was.

MURIEL. Dorcas?

VIVIEN. If Dorcas is taking something, it's nothing to do with me. It's something she's done on her own. She's always wanted to be brightest and best.

JANET. When I was thirteen she used to be my God.

Enter TOM.

TOM. I thought there'd be a surfeit of smiles. I did try and warn you.

HILARY. One out of five?

TOM. I always suspected Ableman was half crazy.

HILARY. How did you get on to it?

TOM. Women rivalling men. There had to be an explanation.

HILARY. There's still Sue's run. Janet's. Muriel's.

JANET. I did run that fast?

VIVIEN. Yes.

Enter DORCAS.

DORCAS. Why?

HILARY. I knew you were a liability.

JANET. You're a cheat.

VIVIEN. Why Dorcas? Why?

DORCAS. Safe you said. Safe.

VIVIEN. I was pretending.

DORCAS. It isn't a game. It isn't a game.

VIVIEN. What I gave you was safe.

HILARY. Do you know how much money you've just poured down a very dirty drain?

DORCAS. Do you know where I got the money.

TOM. Ortolan?

HILARY. This is nothing to do with us.

DORCAS. What about our accounts? I got all sorts of things. I swapped. Couldn't have got it without your money.

SUE. If you wanted to run faster why didn't you just ask her.

DORCAS. If she'd given me two she could have given you two. (*To* VIVIEN). We had a deal. It was safe. Nothing was supposed to show.

VIVIEN. That's because there was nothing there. Anything else you got is due to your own stupidity.

DORCAS. I'm not stupid.

VIVIEN. You went and got more of what I gave you.

SUE. You did give it to us?

VIVIEN. Of what you thought I gave you.

DORCAS. You gave us stuff. I got more. What's the difference? How was I supposed to know it wasn't real?

VIVIEN. Did it never cross your mind?

DORCAS. No, because I'm stupid. All I wanted was to win.

HILARY. How can you possibly call that winning?

TOM. Feet of clay.

DORCAS. You pathetic little man.

PAULINE. Dorcas!

DORCAS. Sniff, sniff, sniff.

TOM. Nothing to do with me. You were dope tested.

DORCAS. Not for months and months. Why today?

TOM. You can't let the flag go up for someone who doesn't play by the rules.

DORCAS. What fucking rules? No one else has any rules. (*She goes at him.*)

MURIEL. Dorcas, don't.

DORCAS *struggles with* TOM.

MURIEL. Leave him.

DORCAS. I'm going to kill him.

MURIEL. Get him out.

VIVIEN *and* HILARY *rescue* TOM. JANET *starts to scream. The other women hold* DORCAS.

HILARY. I can assure you Golden Girls has no part in any of this.

TOM. I suppose I should be thankful it wasn't steroids.

They take him off.

PAULINE (*to* VIVIEN *as they go*). I could have run. If there was something I could have had to calm me down.

Enter LACES. *He has the others' dope testing cards.*

LACES. They're waiting. It's the rules.

Scene Six

The post-mortem

MURIEL. I was frightened. I had to say. Perhaps I should have waited.

DORCAS. I might have been tested anyway.

PAULINE. No one knows if it's true about Lynikova.

SUE. Rumour and counter-rumour. We wanted her to have cheated. None of us believed she could be that good.

JANET. I really believed in Vivien. She shouldn't have played games with us.

MURIEL. We went along with it . . .

SUE. Of course we did, look at our times.

PAULINE. She told us it wouldn't show up.

SUE. We didn't want to know.

MURIEL. We only thought of getting off the next hundredth.

JANET. We were used!

SUE. Of course we were used.

JANET. Vivien.

PAULINE. Tom Billbow's copy.

MURIEL. Ortolan. I'm sorry. You'll never be the Golden Girl now.

SUE. It's Dad you have to explain to. I wouldn't mind staying here in the sun, forever. If we never had to go home.

JANET. It's going to be horrible going home.

MURIEL. We've still got our silvers and our personal bests.

JANET. We'll be banned.

DORCAS. *You* won't.

JANET. But —

DORCAS. You did it, young one. You did it. All of you.

SUE. What about you?

DORCAS. What about me?

Enter LACES.

LACES. I've tried to keep them off your backs for as long as I could. BBC. They've got ten minutes on the satellite. (*The women go.*) Not you. (DORCAS *stops.*) It'll be for life, Dorcas.

DORCAS. For 5 minutes we were the best. Better than the East Germans. Better than anybody. Better than the men. The most perfect there could be. What I'd always wanted. I was pure gold.

LACES. It's a good feeling, isn't it?

DORCAS. Best in the world.

LACES *and* DORCAS *shake hands.* LACES *goes.* DORCAS *takes the dross of the bust. She sings.*

Speak ye comfortably to Jerusalem,
Speak ye comfortably to Jerusalem,
And cry unto her,
That her warfare,
Her warfare is accomplished,
That her iniquity is pardoned,
That her iniquity is pardoned.

Further titles in the Methuen Modern Plays
and World Dramatists series are
described on the following pages.

Barrie Keeffe	*Gimme Shelter (Gem, Gotcha, Getaway)*
	Barbarians (Killing Time, Abide With Me, In the City)
	A Mad World, My Masters
Arthur Kopit	*Indians*
	Wings
Larry Kramer	*The Normal Heart*
John McGrath	*The Cheviot, the Stag and the Black, Black Oil*
David Mamet	*Glengarry Glen Ross*
	American Buffalo
David Mercer	*After Haggerty*
	Cousin Vladimir and *Shooting the Chandelier*
	Duck Song
	The Monster of Karlovy Vary and *Then and Now*
	No Limits To Love
Arthur Miller	*The American Clock*
	The Archbishop's Ceiling
	Two-Way Mirror
	Danger: Memory!
Percy Mtwa Mbongeni Ngema Barney Simon	*Woza Albert!*
Peter Nichols	*Passion Play*
	Poppy
Joe Orton	*Loot*
	What the Butler Saw
	Funeral Games and *The Good and Faithful Servant*
	Entertaining Mr Sloane
	Up Against It
Louise Page	*Golden Girls*
Harold Pinter	*The Birthday Party*
	The Room and *The Dumb Waiter*
	The Caretaker
	A Slight Ache and other plays
	The Collection and *The Lover*

	The Homecoming
	Tea Party and other plays
	Landscape and *Silence*
	Old Times
	No Man's Land
	Betrayal
	The Hothouse
	Other Places (*A Kind of Alaska, Victoria Station, Family Voices*)
Luigi Pirandello	*Henry IV*
	Six Characters in Search of an Author
Sephen Poliakoff	*Coming in to Land*
	Hitting Town and *City Sugar*
	Breaking the Silence
David Rudkin	*The Saxon Shore*
	The Sons of Light
	The Triumph of Death
Jean-Paul Sartre	*Crime Passionnel*
Wole Soyinka	*Madmen and Specialists*
	The Jero Plays
	Death and the King's Horseman
	A Play of Giants
C. P. Taylor	*And a Nighingale Sang . . .*
	Good
Peter Whelan	*The Accrington Pals*
Nigel Williams	*Line 'Em*
	Class Enemy
Theatre Workshop	*Oh What a Lovely War!*
Various authors	*Best Radio Plays of 1978* (Don Haworth: *Episode on a Thursday Evening;* Tom Mallin: *Halt! Who Goes There?;* Jennifer Phillips: *Daughters of Men;* Fay Weldon: *Polaris;* Jill Hyem: *Remember Me;* Richard Harris: *Is It Something I Said?*)
	Best Radio Plays of 1979 (Shirley Gee: *Typhoid Mary;* Carey Harrison: *I Never Killed My German;* Barrie Keeffe: *Heaven Scent;*

John Kirkmorris: *Coxcombe;* John
Peacock: *Attard in Retirement;* Olwen
Wymark: *The Child*)

Best Radio Plays of 1981 (Peter Barnes:
The Jumping Mimuses of Byzantium;
Don Haworth: *Talk of Love and War;*
Harold Pinter: *Family Voices;* David
Pownall: *Beef;* J P Rooney: *The Dead
Image;* Paul Thain: *The Biggest
Sandcastle in the World*)

Best Radio Plays of 1982 (Rhys
Adrian: *Watching the Plays Together;*
John Arden: *The Old Man Sleeps
Alone;* Harry Barton: *Hoopoe Day;*
Donald Chapman: *Invisible Writing;*
Tom Stoppard: *The Dog It Was
That Died;* William Trevor: *Autumn
Sunshine*)

Best Radio Plays of 1983 (Wally K Daly:
Time Slip; Shirley Gee: *Never in My
Lifetime;* Gerry Jones: *The Angels The
Grow Lonely;* Steve May: *No
Exceptions;* Martyn Read: *Scouting for
Boys*)

Best Radio Plays of 1984 (Stephen
Dunstone: *Who Is Sylvia?;* Don
Haworth: *Daybreak;* Robert Ferguson
Transfigured Night; Caryl Phillips:
The Wasted Years; Christopher Russe
Swimmer; Rose Tremain: *Temporary
Shelter*)

Best Radio Plays of 1985 (Rhys
Adrian: *Outpatient;* Barry
Collins: *King Canute;* Martin
Crimp: *The Attempted Acts;*
David Pownall: *Ploughboy
Monday;* James Saunders:
Menocchio; Michael Wall:
Hiroshima: The Movie)

World Dramatists

Collections of plays by the best-known modern playwrights in value-for-money paperbacks.

John Arden	**PLAYS: ONE** *Serjeant Musgrave's Dance, The Workhouse Donkey, Armstrong's Last Goodnight*
Brendan Behan	**THE COMPLETE PLAYS** *The Quare Fellow, The Hostage, Richard's Cork Leg, Moving Out, A Garden Party, The Big House*
Edward Bond	**PLAYS: ONE** *Saved, Early Morning, The Pope's Wedding* **PLAYS: TWO** *Lear, The Sea, Narrow Road to the Deep North, Black Mass, Passion*
Howard Brenton	**PLAYS: ONE** *Christie in Love, Magnificence, The Churchill Play, Weapons of Happiness, Epsom Downs, Sore Throats*
Georg Büchner	**THE COMPLETE PLAYS** *Danton's Death, Leonce and Lena, Woyzeck* with *The Hessian Courier, Lenz, On Cranial Nerves* and *Selected Letters*
Caryl Churchill	**PLAYS: ONE** *Owners, Traps, Vinegar Tom, Light Shining in Buckinghamshire, Cloud Nine*
Noël Coward	**PLAYS: ONE** *Hay Fever, The Vortex, Fallen Angels, Easy Virtue*

PLAYS: THREE
Rosmersholm, The Lady from the Sea, Little Eyolf
PLAYS: FOUR
The Pillars of Society, John Gabriel Borkman, When We Dead Awaken
PLAYS: FIVE
Brand, Emperor and Galilean
PLAYS: SIX
Peer Gynt, The Pretenders

Molière
FIVE PLAYS
The School for Wives, Tartuffe, The Misanthrope, The Miser, The Hypochondriac

Clifford Odets
SIX PLAYS
Waiting for Lefty, Awake and Sing!, Till the Day I Die, Paradise Lost, Golden Boy, Rocket to the Moon

Joe Orton
THE COMPLETE PLAYS
Entertaining Mr Sloane, Loot, What the Butler Saw, The Ruffian on the Stair, The Erpingham Camp, Funeral Games, The Good and Faithful Servant

Arthur Wing Pinero
THREE PLAYS
The Magistrate, The Second Mrs Tanqueray, Trelawny of the 'Wells'

Harold Pinter
PLAYS: ONE
The Birthday Party, The Room, The Dumb Waiter, A Slight Ache, The Hothouse, A Night Out
PLAYS: TWO
The Caretaker, The Dwarfs, The Collection, The Lover, Night School, Trouble in the Works, The Black and White, Request Stop, Last to Go, Special Offer

PLAYS: THREE
The Homecoming, Tea Party, The Basement, Landscape, Silence, That's Your Trouble, That's All, Applicant, Interview, Dialogue for Three, Night

PLAYS: FOUR
Old Times, No Man's Land, Betrayal, Monologue, Family Voices

Luigi Pirandello

THREE PLAYS
The Rules of the Game, Six Characters in Search of an Author, Henry IV

Terence Rattigan

PLAYS: ONE
French Without Tears, The Winslow Boy, The Browning Version, Harlequinade

PLAYS: TWO
The Deep Blue Sea, Separate Tables, In Praise of Love, Before Dawn

Sophocles

THE THEBAN PLAYS
Oedipus the King, Oedipus at Colonus, Antigone

August Strindberg

PLAYS: ONE
The Father, Miss Julie and *The Ghost Sonata*

PLAYS: TWO
A Dream Play, The Dance of Death, The Stronger

Wilde

THREE PLAYS
The Importance of Being Earnest, Lady Windermere's Fan, An Ideal Husband

Synge

THE COMPLETE PLAYS
The Playboy of the Western World,
The Tinker's Wedding, In the Shadow
of the Glen, Riders to the Sea, The
Well of the Saints, Deirdre of the
Sorrows